Build Your
Bounce-Back Ability

Build Your Bounce-Back Ability

NELL WEBB MOHNEY

DIMENSIONS
FOR LIVING
NASHVILLE

BUILD YOUR BOUNCE-BACK ABILITY

Copyright © 2000 by Abingdon Press

This book is printed on acid-free paper.

Library of Congress Cataloging-in-Publication Data

ISBN 0-687-09830-0

00 01 02 03 04 05 06 07 08 09—10 9 8 7 6 5 4 3 2 1

MANUFACTURED IN THE UNITED STATES OF AMERICA

To

my good friends Joe and Carol Jensen Harding,

who have bounced back from tragedy, serious illness, and

divorce with courage and faith.

Their bounce-back ability has inspired and encouraged all of

us who know them.

Contents

Introduction

I once watched a crocus and a jonquil "bounce back" after a winter of darkness and cold temperatures. It occurred to me that one of the evidences of our well-being is the ability to bounce back after we experience the darkness of disappointment, failure, or tragedy. How is *your* bounce-back ability?

At a conference I attended, the speaker gave a graphic demonstration of how people respond to problems and stress. He used an egg, an apple, an orange, and a tennis ball. First, he dropped the egg. Fortunately, it was in a sealable plastic bag. The moment the egg hit the floor, it broke and splattered all over the inside of the bag. The speaker indicated that some people are like that. Whether experiencing failure or disappointment, they are shattered, broken, unable to bounce back.

Then he dropped a large, ruby red apple. When the apple hit the platform, it didn't splatter; it just rolled on. To look at the apple from a distance, you would see no obvious bruises. Upon closer observation, however, you would realize that although the apple kept rolling, it had sustained numerous bruises. Many people are like that. When they have been knocked down, they continue to go through the motions of living. They get out of bed, get dressed, go to work, and perform their responsibilities—though perfunctorily. To the casual observer, there are no obvious bruises. If you know the person well, however, it is apparent that he or she has sustained so many bruises that there is no bounce-back ability.

The third object the speaker dropped was an orange. It fell to the floor with a thud. It stopped instantly—no rolling for the orange. Even when he picked it up, there were no bruises on its thick skin. Yet we knew the impact was so great that there had to be bruises—on the inside. Some people don't shatter when tragedy occurs. They simply put their lives on hold. The result is depression, withdrawal, and an inability to move forward.

Then came the tennis ball. The harder the ball hit the floor, the higher it bounced. It had true bounce-back ability!

Like the tennis ball, *our* bounce-back ability is determined by what we have on the inside—our skills, our "absorption ability," and our faith. I am convinced that the following principles enable us to absorb the hurt more easily and move forward.

First, identify the problem. A man told me once that he was losing his job because he had inadequate job skills. The truth was that he was completely competent in the performance of his duties, but he had difficulty working with others. He needed to learn interpersonal skills in order to be a good team member.

Second, see your problem in perspective. We should remember that being a part of the human race means that we will have problems. Jesus said, "In the world [you] shall have tribulation" (John 16:33 KJV). Remember that other people have gone through similar situations and have bounced back. Don't bog down in self-pity.

Third, talk over your feelings with a trusted friend or counselor who can be objective. There is a positive aspect to every situation. Don't focus on what you have lost but on what you have left. What happens to you is not as important as how you react to what happens.

Fourth, determine whether it is better for you to hold on and "ride out the storm" or to let go and accept what cannot be changed. If an era has passed, then work at moving on.

Finally, remember that real bounce-back ability comes from a daily relationship with the living God. He is the one who, through his love and grace, offers us a second chance. With God, nothing is impossible. With God, you can build your bounce-back ability!

Chapter 1

Build Your Bounce-Back Ability

[Christ] has said, "I will never leave you or forsake you."

—Hebrews 13:5

The rain was coming down in torrents as the small EMB 120 Brazilia plane tried to land in Albany, Georgia. Seated near the front, I overheard one flight attendant say to another who was flying as a passenger, "Two unsuccessful attempts, and I don't believe we will make it this time. The pilot says that if we don't land this time, we'll go back to Macon."

My mind was racing. *Oh no!* I thought. *My speaking engagement in Albany is only an hour from now. If we don't make it now, I'll never get back in time.* As I peered through the rain-splattered window, I suddenly had a flashback to two months earlier when torrential rain from tropical storm Alberto had caused the flood of the century for the people of Southwestern and South Central Georgia. On that July afternoon, residents had heard on radio and television these frightening words as the banks of the Flint River began to overflow: "This is not a drill. Please evacuate your home immediately. Take as few of your belongings as possible. Your home may soon be underwater. Act quickly. I repeat: This is not a drill."

I hope this is not a repeat of that July day, I thought as my plane finally made a bumpy landing. The people of Albany had not been as fortunate. The Flint River had crested at a record forty-four feet, and seven thousand residents had lost their homes—less than five hundred of whom had flood insurance. Though only four people had actually lost their lives, the flood had created a tragedy of major proportions: 4,202 persons were housed in thirty-three shelters; 2,002 persons were out of work as a result of the flood; there were 160 interruptions in the state highway system; and 400 caskets were dislodged from the cemeteries and had to be recovered and identified. Yet two months later these brave, stalwart citizens had moved ahead with hope and determination. That's called bounce-back ability!

Somehow all of those people were personified for me in "Mary," a retired school teacher who lost her home and all its furnishings. Though there was sadness in her voice as she told me her story, there was no trace of self-pity. An attractive, well-educated, pleasant woman, Mary had bought her small brick home on a tree-lined street in Albany thirty years ago. She had added on to the house when her elderly parents came to live with her. Following their deaths and her retirement, Mary felt that she was happily settled for the rest of her life. Her house was paid for, she had a modest pension, and she was actively involved in church and community affairs.

Before those two fateful days in early July, she had celebrated the Fourth of July holiday with a friend and was not too concerned about the news that Hurricane Alberto seemed to be stationary over Georgia. After all, she lived on a city street six miles from the Flint River, and her area was always several feet above the one-hundred-year flood level. Yet what she didn't know was that there was a two-mile area in Albany—imperceptible to the eye—that was in a slight indentation. When the flood waters moved from the river banks through the county, they settled into that indentation. Friends who lived on the same street only two blocks away from the low area were not flooded at all.

Unfortunately, Mary's home was in the low area. When the flood waters reached her yard, she moved her car to higher ground and returned to pack a small bag and put some additional things in a plastic bag. "I felt like a bag lady as I was rescued by boat and taken to the home of a friend," she said with tears misting her eyes. "Even then I expected to be back in my home shortly."

It was two weeks before she was able to return to her home. With the first look at the interior, the enormousness of her loss was apparent. Clothing was ruined, furniture was completely destroyed, mud covered the floors, and the stench was almost unbearable. She realized that she had neither the money (no flood insurance) nor the spirit to rebuild this house of her dreams.

When I talked with Mary, she had sold her home at a fraction of its worth and was renting a small apartment. Yet she had bounced back in her perspective and in her spirit. I asked what had helped her. "It was three F's: faith, family, and friends," she replied.

Mary's Christian faith helped her to work through her grief and reminded her that every ending can have a new beginning. Her church established a shelter in their gym, and though she stayed with a friend and didn't need the services, it was comforting to know they were available. Her church also provided a sense of continuity and structure during the upheaval. The flood had come on a Thursday, and on Sunday morning she attended her Sunday school class and later sat on her usual pew for worship. The words of a hymn they sang that day had special meaning for her: "Change and decay in all around I see; O Thou who changest not, abide with me."

Mary's friends, most of whom attend her church, provided not only the loving support anyone needs in a tragedy, but also the physical labor to help Mary clean up the mess. "I will never take friends or family for granted again," she declared.

Though neither her sister nor her brother lives in Albany, they both were "there" for her, helping her talk through the difficult decisions and move on with her life. It was her brother, a minister in New York, who confirmed her unspoken desire to leave her home and begin anew. "You will have many happy memories of your years in that house," he said. "But that was yesterday, and this is today. Leave yesterday behind, and move on with God's help."

Three F's—faith, family, and friends—provide the network for bouncing back from tragedy. Do you have these three requisites to building bounce-back ability?

Steps to Building Bounce-Back Ability

1. Practice flexibility regularly. For example, don't drive to work, the shopping mall, or the church the same way each time. Look for new scenes, new beauty, new construction.

2. Broaden your circle of friends. Keep the old friends, but make some new ones in different age groups. Your life will be greatly enriched through friendships with children, youth, peers, and persons older than you. You can make new friends of all ages by participating in new activities or invit-

---

ing people to your home. I know a ninety-year-old woman who seems ageless. Each year she has a Christmas tea to which she invites people of all age groups. We enjoy it so much that we save the first Friday in December each year for our friend.

3. Remember that Jesus said, "In the world you face persecution. But take courage; I have conquered the world" (John 16:33). No one is exempt, so don't expect a life with no problems.

4. If you expect family members and friends to "be there" for you in your difficulties, then you will need to "be there" for them.

5. Stay "prayed up." Cultivate your faith by living daily in the presence of Christ and continuing to grow through prayer, meditation, study, and worship.

Chapter 2

Get Free from Clutter

Do not be conformed to this world, but be transformed by the renewing of your minds.

—Romans 12:2

---

*R*ush! Hurry! Clutter! Excess! These words flash into my mind many times during the Christmas holidays. Too many activities, too much to do, too little time to savor the meaning of the season. Indeed, instead of feeling refreshed and ready for a brand new year, it is easy to feel jaded. Often by the time I reach New Year's Day, my body is tired of rich food and fancy desserts. I long for simple foods—boiled eggs, baked potatoes, and even the traditional black-eyed peas and greens for New Year's Day.

Thinking about this common "after Christmas" attitude reminds me of an incident that happened in 1974 when my husband, Ralph, and I were taking two tour groups to Oberammergau, Germany, to see the Passion Play during its anniversary year. We planned to take one group, and our son would return with them. Two weeks later, a minister friend, Dr. Elton Jones, would bring the second group and join us in Frankfort, Germany. Ralph and I would be gone for a month. As a result, I packed for every conceivable situation—hot days; cold days;

rainy days; coughing, sneezing days. My suitcase was bulging. Even sitting on top of it didn't help to close it.

In frustration, I thought to myself, *This suitcase is symbolic of my life. I need to simplify, eliminate some activities, clear my focus, and learn to enjoy life more.* So right then I stopped to list five steps to help me accomplish just that. Often when the clutter accumulates and my focus is fuzzy, I remember and review these steps and return to the basics. Maybe they will be of help to you, too.

First, start the day with God. In the early seventies, the author of the book *The First Four Minutes* suggested that when we meet someone for the first time, the first four minutes determine whether or not we will pursue the relationship. Also, the first four minutes when a family gathers after school and work determine the climate for the evening.

After reading that book, it occurred to me that the first four minutes after we awaken allow us to "set our sails" for the day. So when I awaken, instead of thinking how much I have to do and becoming anxious, I condition my mind with gratitude and praise. I begin with my favorite Bible verse: "This is the day that the Lord has made; let us rejoice and be glad in it" (Psalm 118:24). Then I express gratitude to God for all my blessings. When I practice this simple regimen before getting out of bed to exercise and have a quiet time, I begin the day with a sense of calmness and peace.

Second, set realistic and clearly defined goals. Unless your priorities and goals are clear, you will be easily distracted or take on more than you can do. Most time experts suggest that you set three or four big goals for the year, and then determine steps you will need to take within the next thirty days to move toward those goals. Also, learning to plan your week on Sunday helps you to bring the future into the present.

Remember that some of your goals will change as circumstances change, or as you change your mind. After all, goals are not irrevocable; they are tools to focus your life.

Third, regularly renew your mind. Have you ever noticed the intensity on people's faces as you walk down the street? The media's running commentary on violence, crime, and other ills of our society deflates our spirits. Add to that our own personal problems, and it is easy to see why we often feel overwhelmed. We need to remember the words of the apostle Paul: "Do not be conformed to this world, but be transformed by the *renewing of your minds*" (Romans 12:2, emphasis added). We can renew our minds by reading scripture and inspirational literature; and by worshiping, exercising, listening to beautiful music, being in the out-of-doors, looking for beauty, nurturing loving relationships, laughing, and having fun. I like this thought, which I once saw on a party napkin: "He or she who laughs, lasts." Keep your perspective. Remember, thankfully, that God, not you, is in charge of the world.

Fourth, learn to say "no" without feeling guilty. People who have a great need to please others have a hard time with this one. They take on more than they can manage and end up feeling frustrated and angry. It is much easier to say "no" when your goals are clear. In addition to saying "no" to activities, be sure to say "no" to unmanageable debt. It will rob you of peace of mind. Financial consultants say that if you can't discipline yourself to pay off your charge cards every month, you should cut them up.

Fifth, set aside one day each week for worship, rest, and relaxation. As a society, we have disregarded—to our own peril—the commandment to keep the Sabbath holy. One Easter Sunday, the *USA Weekend* magazine cover story was an article adapted from Walter Muller's

Sabbath: Remembering the Sacred Rhythm of Rest and Delight. In the article, Muller said: "Much of modern life is specifically designed to seduce our attention away from Sabbath rest—[and] because we do not rest, we lose our way." To avoid burnout, we must regularly renew our spirits through worship and our bodies through rest and relaxation.

Are you feeling frustrated, overwhelmed, depressed? Is it the clutter of your life that is causing you to feel this way? Choose to simplify and enjoy life more. Remember, this process begins with a decision. Follow these five simple steps and see if they won't simplify and empower your life!

 Steps for Breaking Free from Clutter

1. Set your sails each morning by starting the day with God. Bishop Ralph Cushman's poem "I Met God in the Morning" ends with these lines:

> You must meet Him in the morning,
> If you want Him through the day.

2. Set and stay focused on realistic, clearly defined goals. Remember that goals are not irrevocable; they are tools to focus your life.
3. Regularly renew your mind through laughter, fun, beauty, music, scripture, inspirational literature, worship, exercise, nature, and loving relationships.
4. Learn to say "no" without feeling guilty.
5. Set aside one day each week for worship, rest, and relaxation. Keep the Sabbath Day holy.

Chapter 3

Lighten Up with Laughter

A cheerful heart is a good medicine, but a downcast spirit dries up the bones.

—Proverbs 17:22

She looked like an army drill sergeant. She had a sturdy build, her speech was abrupt, and she had a "take charge," no-nonsense manner. This waitress in an airport restaurant charged through the kitchen door and approached her customers with an "I need your order now" attitude.

That morning one of her customers was a mild-mannered, distinguished looking minister who had been the featured speaker at a large gathering in the city the day before. He was taking an early morning flight back to his home. I happen to know this minister, and he is an extremely articulate person with a delightful sense of humor and an ability to express his thoughts with poetic imagery. On that particular morning, he may have been sleepy or preoccupied with thoughts of his day's activities. At any rate, the burly waitress must have perceived him as tense, even dour, because as she descended on his table she said in a loud, gruff voice, "Lighten up, buttercup!"

When I heard the minister tell this story at a large

gathering, I and all the other participants were convulsed with laughter. In the first place, the thought of such a distinguished gentleman being called "buttercup" was so ludicrous that it was funny. Even more humorous was the fact that he told it on himself—and with such vivid description that we could almost see that substantial woman and smell the coffee she poured as she made that impertinent remark. To be sure, there is a subtle but wonderful benefit that comes from the ability to laugh at ourselves. It helps us to see ourselves in proper perspective—to realize that no matter what our credentials, we are not the center of the universe.

In a world full of pressures and deadlines, most of us would do well to lighten up and laugh more. We continue to learn more and more about the value of laughter. From medical science we have learned that a hearty laugh serves as aerobic exercise for our internal organs. Researchers from Duke University Medical Center say in their report "Aging and God" that laughter has the effect of "internal jogging." We also have learned that laughter improves our circulation and heart rate and lowers our blood pressure. In his book *The Anatomy of an Illness*, Dr. Norman Cousins witnesses to the curative power of laughter in his own life-threatening illness. Part of his rehabilitation regimen was to rent old Laurel and Hardy movies and watch them for several hours each day. Not only was this a distraction from pain and a spirit lifter, but it actually seemed to strengthen his immune system.

Motivational speaker and author Mamie McCullough of Dallas, Texas, has a marvelous ability to see humor in everyday events. She endears herself to her readers and audiences by her ability to laugh at herself. I once heard her tell this funny story. She said that after she speaks, she usually likes to go to the restroom, freshen up, and then get something to eat. When she speaks in Texas, she drives to her engagements; and her habit is to stop at the nearest McDonalds after speaking. Through many such stops, she has learned that the ladies' restrooms at McDonalds in Texas are always on the right. Her stops became so habitual that she didn't even look at the sign on the door. One day after speaking in an adjacent state, she literally ran into a nearby McDonalds. Automatically she turned into the restroom on the right. To her amazement, six men were in the room! When telling about the incident, she said, "I don't know why I felt I ought to explain, but I did. The only thing I could think of to say was, "My husband just left me, and I am looking everywhere for him." What comic relief for a bad situation!

It has been my observation that people who are able to laugh easily are less judgmental, less nervous, less uptight, less gloomy, and less negative. Likewise, they generally are more understanding, more fun to be with, and much more flexible.

Several years ago I went to hear a well-known woman speaker. I had worked hard to clear my schedule and allow enough time for the trip to Knoxville, Tennessee, where she was speaking. When I returned home, my husband asked eagerly, "Well, how did you like her? Did you enjoy the speech?"

Sadly I had to admit, "Ralph, I agreed with everything she said, but the whole experience was a downer. It was too intense! She never smiled, laughed, or even told a humorous incident. As a result, I was exhausted by the end of the hour." Granted, I, and perhaps most of the women present, needed to confront some of the truths she presented that day; but as the song goes, "A spoonful of sugar helps the medicine go down." A little bit of laughter that day would have made the truths much easier to accept.

One of my favorite Bible stories is that of an aged Abraham and Sarah doubled up with laughter on being told they were to have a baby. Even God laughed with them. They later named their "miracle child" Isaac, which means "laughter." I have often thought that the Creator of the universe must laugh when we strut around with feelings of imperial self-importance and self-sufficiency. The Creator must be more saddened than amused, however, when we forget our dependence on him; or when we forget that we, like Abraham and Sarah, can accomplish unbelievable things when we claim his promises and seek to fulfill his purposes. Perhaps many of us need to hear God say to us: "Lighten up, buttercup! Lighten up with laughter!"

Steps for Lightening Up with Laughter

1. Read a good health magazine to confirm the importance of laughter to our physical health. (Recommendations: *The University of California, Berkeley, Wellness Letter,* published monthly by Health Letter Associates, P. O. Box 420148, Palm Coast, FL, 32142, and *Harvard Women's Health Watch,* published monthly by the Harvard Medical School Health Publications Group, 164 Longwood Avenue, Boston, MA, 02115.)
2. Acknowledge that you are not in charge of the universe. This allows you to turn loose your need to control people and circumstances.
3. Become intentional about looking for humor in everyday life.
4. Learn a good joke or funny story and be ready to

tell it at an appropriate time. Try it out on your friends to see if it's really funny.

5. Become intentional about relaxing and expressing gratitude. These two things will help you enjoy life more.

6. Understand that joy is actually a fruit of the Holy Spirit living within you; so stay close to Christ, the Master of joy (see Galatians 5:22-23).

Chapter 4

Develop a Contagious Aura

[Jesus] said to him, "You shall love the Lord your God with all your heart, and with all your soul, and with all your mind."

—*Matthew 22:37*

---

*E*ach person seated in the room, waiting for the seminar to begin, saw her that day. She looked as if she were in her early twenties. She was average height, average weight, and average in every aspect of outward appearance; yet she was totally appealing. There was an aliveness about her. She exuded energy and interest, joy in being alive, and an openness to others. Though I had heard that we all have an aura of personality, I had never seen it so vividly as I did that day. The quotations I had heard so often began to make sense to me: "What you are speaks so loudly, I cannot hear what you say" (Ralph Waldo Emerson); "The medium is the message" (Marshall McLuhan); "As [a man] thinketh in his heart, so *is* he" (Proverbs 23:7 KJV); "We are not responsible for the face we are born with, but we are responsible for the face we die with" (E. Stanley Jones).

Since that day in 1978, I have read everything I can find about personalities and the auras they create. Webster defines *aura* as "a subtle emanation." Teenagers might call it "vibes" (vibrations). The more I have read and observed, the more I am convinced that we all create an aura, or a climate, wherever we are—in our homes, at school, at work, in our social settings, and in our churches.

From my observations and my interviews with well over one hundred persons who have strong, positive auras—including the young woman at the seminar who entered the room so radiantly—I have discovered that the following things combine to determine an individual's aura: self-image, outward appearance, thoughts, attitudes, relational skills, and a core commitment or value system. Without exception, the one attribute that all of my interviewees have had in common is a strong value system based on the Judeo-Christian faith. More particularly, over half of them have been practicing, committed Christians. A story told by Dr. Fred Craddock, professor of homiletics at the Candler School of Theology, Emory University, symbolizes the core commitment of those persons.

While Dr. Craddock was a seminary student at Princeton University, Gorman Williams, a missionary from India, came to speak at a chapel service. He told the seminarians of an experience that happened in 1945. He had purchased a ticket for a long-awaited furlough back to the States. Some time later, he heard of some Jews who had escaped from Germany and had come by boat to India, hoping to find refuge. The Indian government would not allow them to immigrate there, but they did grant permission for the Jews to stay a short time in the lofts of buildings along the dock. The refugees were living in cramped, inhumane conditions.

It was Christmas Eve when Williams heard about the Jews. He went immediately to the dock, entered the first building, and called out, "Merry Christmas! What would you like for Christmas?"

They replied, "We're Jewish."

"I know," Williams said, "but what would you like for Christmas?"

"We would like some German pastries," replied the weary Jews.

After selling his ticket to America, Williams purchased German pastries—lots and lots of them; large baskets full. As Williams told the story, one brash, judgmental, young freshman stood and reprimanded the missionary: "You shouldn't have done that. They were not even Christians."

"No, they weren't, but I am," the missionary replied quietly. (From a 1993 sermon given by Dick Wills at Christ United Methodist Church in Fort Lauderdale.)

The people who are making a strong, positive difference in our world today are those who have a core commitment, or an inner gyroscope, which enables them to navigate the rapids of life with peace and confidence. They are not centered in themselves but are rooted and grounded in the God who created the universe and who, through Christ, offers eternal life to all who seek it. This core commitment determines their perception of the universe, of their fellow human beings, of relationships, and even of time. My observation is that they have learned to live fully in the "now" and to lean forward into the future rather than reliving the past.

These are the people who have discovered that the way "out" is "in." They have an inner strength that comes from commitment to eternal purposes, and to One far bigger than themselves. As a result, they exude a confident, hopeful aura that is appealingly contagious.

What kind of aura are you developing?

Steps to Developing a Contagious Aura

1. Have a positive self-image. This comes best when you internalize your Christian heritage: made in the image of God, redeemed by Jesus Christ, and empowered by the Holy Spirit.

2. Remember that your core commitment or value system, determined by your religious faith or lack of it, is easily discernable to others. Your treatment of them is the quickest evidence they see.

3. Relate to others in a pleasant, non-competitive way. This, perhaps more than anything else, affects the way others perceive you.

4. Choose to have a positive attitude. Your attitude tells others whether you are friendly and accepting or bitter and angry.

5. Be well-groomed and appropriately dressed for all occasions. This has nothing to do with the cost of your clothes; it has to do with grooming—clothes pressed, shoes polished, and so forth. Mary Kay Ashe told me in an interview that she once said to a convention group of women, "There is no such thing as an ugly woman—only a lazy one." The same applies to men as well.

Chapter 5

Don't Procrastinate

So teach us to count our days that we may gain a wise heart.

—*Psalm 90:12*

---

*P*rofessional thieves are often clever and cunning, and some are even charming. "Lucas" was all three. Years ago he drove into our small, unassuming town and took it by storm. Like Robert Preston playing the role of Harold Hill in the movie *The Music Man*, he quickly became a part of community life—joining a church, a service club, and the chamber of commerce. Children and youth thought he was great fun, and adults thought he was wonderful.

Lucas sold encyclopedias, and that in itself should have been a tip-off. Usually it was college students who sold encyclopedias, but Lucas was thirty-two. We should have known better. I heard a story about a man who was asked if he wanted to buy a set of encyclopedias. He said calmly, "No, thank you. We have a teenager who knows everything." We should have used that reply! But we hadn't heard that clever reply, and Lucas absconded with thousands of dollars from our citizens. When the city fathers tried to catch him, they discovered that he had more aliases than a dog has fleas. He was a big-time thief!

There is a thief all of us deal with almost daily. He is just as believable as Lucas yet even more subtle. His name is procrastination. He doesn't steal money or silver or TV sets; he steals our time, our motivation, our very lives. In their place he leaves excuses, alibis, rationalizations, and guilt. We often don't see through his ruses until it is too late. Like most crooks, this pro hits us when we are weak or when we relax our defenses.

Say, for example, that you have promised your children you will help them build a playhouse on Saturday morning. You awaken with every intention of doing so, but procrastination reminds you that you have had a terrible week—that you are exhausted and deserve to relax. There is no suggestion from the thief that you refuse to build the playhouse, only that you postpone it until you are rested. The result: Your children's trust in you erodes (especially since this has happened before), you waste time during most of the day, and you end the day feeling guilty.

Or, let's say that your bathroom scales tell an unhappy story. You know that, for your health's sake, you must reduce your caloric intake and cut back on fat and sugar. Today is the day to begin, but the thief whispers the magic word *mañana*. He says, "Tomorrow is the time to begin because today will be stressful." So you reach for another pastry, and the grim thief has won another battle. You have succumbed to Scarlett O'Hara's philosophy: "I will worry about that tomorrow."

Procrastination robs us of our ability to be decisive. Obviously any weighty decision should not be made without thoughtful consideration and prayer. Yet some people spend their lives "sitting on the fence," paralyzed into inaction. As a result, they sit on the sidelines of the game of life, wasting their energy and talents. When they put off a decision about a problem that needs to be solved, the problem grows larger.

Several years ago I presented a series of seminars for a particular company. The CEO of this company had a bud vase on his handsome desk. Instead of holding a rose, as one might expect, the bud vase held a thorn-filled branch. When I asked why, he told me it was a reminder that problems need to be faced promptly and decisively. "If you touch the thorns tentatively, they will prick you," he said. "If, however, you grasp them quickly and all at once, they don't hurt at all." Actually I didn't try that, so I don't know whether it's true or not; but I am certain that when we postpone facing our problems, they become stickier and more difficult to handle.

In my own life, I have found that I receive "divine nudges" prompting me to help someone or to express appreciation or to take some constructive action. When I disregard the nudges, I always regret it. I am still sad over the fact that I didn't take the time to tell my paternal grandmother how much she had influenced my life. She knew that I loved her, but I never expressed in words what she meant to me. Though I knew she wasn't feeling well, I had no idea that she was near death. So, I allowed the thief to rob me of an opportunity I could never have again.

If procrastination is your problem, the way to defeat it is by decisive action *now*. In the words of the Nike commercial, "Just do it." The Sanskrit reminds us that "Today well lived makes every yesterday a happy memory and every tomorrow a vision of loveliness. Look well then to this day."

Steps to Overcoming Procrastination

1. Decide that you will not put off until tomorrow what needs to be done today.

2. Start with simple steps in your attempt to be more decisive.

• Give yourself a deadline for making a decision.

• Write a list of things that need to be done or considered before the final decision.

• Make a decision by the appointed time. Don't waffle!

• Don't worry if you make a mistake. It isn't the end of the world, and making a mistake is better than living in indecision.

3. Recognize that lack of motivation often comes from lethargy and fear. We overcome lethargy by becoming more purposeful and organized. We overcome fear by increasing our faith and courageously doing the thing we fear.

4. Remember that you are not a spectator in life but a player in the thick of the game.

5. Resolve to be a part of the solution of life's problems. One of the best ways to do this is to write down a problem about which you are concerned. Think and pray about it during your quiet time, and write down one action, however small, that you can take to make a positive difference. Then do it! This will relieve your frustration and feelings of helplessness and help you to overcome procrastination.

Chapter 6

Be Sure You Are on the Right Bus

"I am the way, and the truth, and the life. No one comes to the Father except through me."

—John 14:6

---

*T*he late Dr. Harry Emerson Fosdick, former minister of the Riverside Church of New York City, once recounted the story of a man who boarded a bus in New York with the intention of going to Detroit. As he stepped from the bus at the end of the long trip, he asked for directions to Woodward Avenue. When he was told there was no Woodward Avenue, he was indignant. He knew Detroit, and he knew there was a Woodward Avenue. So, he protested the people's inhospitable failure to direct him. It was some time before he could face the fact that despite the clarity of his desire and intention, he was not in Detroit. Actually, he was in Kansas City. He had taken the wrong bus!

We are often like that man. We know what we want in life and what we intend to do, but our daily actions take us in a different direction. If we say we want a fit, healthy body but eat foods that clog our arteries; refuse to exercise; become addicted to food, alcohol, drugs, or tobacco; or live in a tense state of worry, we are "on the wrong bus." If we say we want a good marriage but don't allow time for listening to our spouse—for honestly sharing our thoughts and feelings and letting our inner worlds touch—then we are "on the wrong bus." If we say we want to be all that we were created to be but don't make time to search for our potential and take advantage of growth opportunities, then we are "on the wrong bus." If we say we want to grow spiritually but don't have regular times for worship, prayer, and study of the Bible and great spiritual classics, then we are "on the wrong bus." If we want to be close to our children but don't spend time doing things together with them—working, playing, laughing, sharing, worshiping—then we are "on the wrong bus."

Perhaps you are saying, "Wait a minute! I can't possibly do all those things. After all, nobody is perfect." You're right: Nobody's perfect. I never say those words without remembering a friend of mine. He was the minister of a small rural church where people felt free to ask questions or make comments during the sermon. One morning the pastor was talking about how we all need the grace of God because, he said, "nobody's perfect." At that point, a sixty-year-old man raised his hand. The pastor was shocked and asked, "Mr. Ridley, you mean you think you are perfect?" The man replied, "No, pastor. But from the way my wife talks about her first husband, he must have been."

Obviously, only God is perfect, but God has created us to live far more abundantly than most of us live. The truly great and successful people I have known and read about seem to have several characteristics in common.

First, successful people have a dream for their lives—and great expectations. They believe firmly in their dream and are able to visualize it, stay focused on it, discipline themselves for whatever steps are needed to accomplish it, and always remain loyal to their highest ideals. Gladstone, the eminent English statesman from 1832–1895, was asked the secret of his successful career. He replied with one word: *concentration*. When we make a decision to stay focused on our dreams or plans, we give up vagueness and generalities.

Second, successful people count the cost of their dream. They ask what additional things they will have to do—or what things they will have to give up—to accomplish the dream. It was Jesus who said, "Which of you, intending to build a tower, does not first sit down and estimate the cost, to see whether he has enough to complete it?" (Luke 14:28). Certainly, there is nothing more important than building our lives and our destinies.

Third, successful people set goals. They not only dream but also plan the action steps they will take to accomplish their dreams. Rather than expecting to take all the steps at once, they break them down into short-range goals (goals for one day to one month), long-range goals (goals for several months to several years), and ultimate goals (lifelong goals). Ultimate goals indicate what an individual wants his or her life to represent at the end of life's earthly journey. Or, as Stephen Covey writes in his book *The Seven Habits of Highly Effective People*, "Begin with the end in mind."

Listing your ultimate goals will take time, thought, evaluation, and prayer. Don't list more than six ultimate goals. Then, under each one, list as many additional goals as you choose. After months of thinking and praying about my own ultimate goals, I came up with four: (1) to be an authentic Christian; (2) to give and receive love, particularly to my significant others; (3) to use my talents of speaking and writing to glorify God and help others; and (4) to go to heaven when I die. Then I began to work on a list of short- and long-term goals that would move me in the direction of my ultimate goals. One of my short-term goals, for example, is to do something each day that helps me grow spiritually—and thus moves me toward achieving my first and fourth ultimate goals. A long-term goal is to listen to extraordinary speakers—either in person or on tape—in order to learn from them. Likewise, I can take courses in communications to refine my writing and speaking.

In my own experience, life seems much easier since I decided to outline on Sunday afternoon the tasks I need to accomplish each day in order to reach my short-term goal for that week. A "to do" list can keep each of us focused on our dreams and our priorities—which are, after all, what prevent us from getting on the wrong bus.

Dreaming the dream is not too difficult, but the fruition of that dream hinges on our ability to "keep on keeping on." Maybe that is one of the things Jesus meant when he said, "The gate is narrow and the road is hard that leads to life, and there are few who find it" (Matthew 7:14). No one dreams of failing. We don't intend to go in that direction. The prodigal son didn't intend to end up in a pigpen. The alcoholics I have known never set out to be alcoholics. In the hundreds of weddings I have attended, I have never known a bride and groom to stand at the altar and dream of divorce. Yet in our everyday actions, however, many of us simply take the wrong bus. The words of Dr. W. L. Ewing are a reminder to us all: "What I am to be, I am now becoming." *So be sure you're on the right bus!*

Steps to "Getting on the Right Bus"

1. Dream a big dream, visualize it, and stay focused on it.

2. Count the cost of accomplishing your dream. Determine what you will have to do and/or give up in order to make your dream a reality.

3. Set goals for the accomplishment of your dream.

4. Make a "to do" list for your daily actions.

5. Be aware of the danger of letting your actions take you in the opposite direction from your goals and dreams. (For example, if you want to be physically fit, you must eat nutritionally, exercise regularly, and learn to manage stress.)

6. Persevere in your goals—in other words, "keep on keeping on."

7. Remember that what you are to be, you are now becoming.

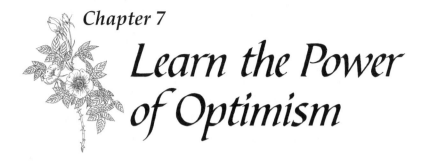

Chapter 7

Learn the Power of Optimism

"In the world you face persecution. But take courage; I have conquered the world!"

—*John 16:33*

Seeing our local theater's production of *Annie* reminded me of the power of optimism. Broadway couldn't have done a better production! The sets were wonderfully realistic—from the orphanage to Daddy Warbucks' mansion—and the cast was superb, especially the children. When the young girl who played the role of Annie sang "You can bet your bottom dollar that the sun will come up tomorrow," she reminded her listeners of the constancy of God's creation. It was easy to see how her optimism created hope in the people around her.

For most of my life, I believed that one's outlook on life came as "standard equipment." I thought that optimists were born with genes for a happy, sunny disposition, whereas pessimists were born with genes for a melancholic, sensitive, introverted temperament. Obviously, genetic and environmental factors do influence us, but God endowed us with wonderful capabilities that lift us far above the stimulus-and-response level. These capabilities include self-awareness, imagination, conscience, and independent will. They give us the freedom we need to choose. This makes us "a little lower than the angels, . . . crowned . . . with glory and honour" (Psalm 8:5 KJV).

Austrian psychiatrist Viktor Frankl learned that even in the degrading, repugnant, inhumane conditions of a Nazi concentration camp, he had the freedom to choose his reactions. He called this our ultimate, God-given freedom. Whatever happens to us, we have the freedom to choose how we will respond.

For Christians, optimism comes from the joyful knowledge that we are loved and forgiven by God. When we accept this gift of love, revealed in Jesus Christ (John 3:16), we are empowered for living in the here and now. We know that difficulties will come, but we can see them as temporary challenges rather than as permanent problems. Jesus told us, "In the world you face persecution. But take courage; I have conquered the world!" (John 16:33).

Over the past three decades, the findings of outstanding psychiatrists have helped us understand that optimism and pessimism are learned. Dr. Martin E. P. Seligman, professor of psychiatry at the University of Pennsylvania, says that optimism and pessimism are learned from our primary caregiver (usually mother) in the first seven years of life. But that's not the end of the story; we can change our "programming"! In his book *The Power of Optimism*, Dr. Alan Loy McGinnis suggests that optimists share twelve characteristics. From these characteristics, I have developed my own list of twelve important habits of an optimist. I offer them to you here as a "blueprint" for becoming a lifelong optimist.

Give yourself a "check-up." Are you an optimist or a pessimist? Do you know the power of optimism? If not, determine today to learn it and live it!

Steps to Becoming an Optimist

Always remember that, for Christians, optimism comes from the knowledge that we are loved and forgiven by God. When we receive this gift of love, revealed in Jesus Christ (John 3:16), we are empowered for confident, optimistic living!

1. See yourself as a problem solver.
2. Learn to chip away at problems and not be overwhelmed by their enormity.
3. Be confident you can make a difference.
4. Take time to "recharge" your batteries—physically, mentally, and spiritually.
5. Counteract negative thoughts by finding a more positive way of thinking.
6. Look for the kernel of good in bad situations.
7. Visualize victories and happy outcomes.
8. Know the difference between being joyful and being happy, and be joyful even during difficult times.
9. Consistently set new goals rather than rest on old laurels.
10. Look for ways to fill your life with love—through people, causes, ideas, and activities.
11. Do not focus on bad news, and do not gossip.
12. Endorse and live by the prayer of Reinhold Niebuhr: "God, give us grace to accept with serenity the things that cannot be changed, courage to change the things which should be changed, and the wisdom to distinguish the one from the other."

Chapter 8

Develop Staying Power

I have fought the good fight, I have finished the race, I have kept the faith.

—2 Timothy 4:7

---

*I*t was the summer of 1968. The whole world seemed to have "Olympic fever," and I, along with millions, watched via television an unforgettable marathon race that took place in Mexico City.

A large number of well-trained runners from almost every continent gathered at the starting line. The gun sounded, and the twenty-six-mile race was underway. It ended, of course, in the Olympic stadium, where thousands cheered as the medals—bronze, silver, and gold— were presented to each of the winners as his or her national anthem was played and the national flag was raised. It was almost an hour later, after people had turned their attention to other events, that there was an audible murmur going through the crowd. A reporter told the TV audience that the marathon was not yet over. A runner was still on the course. He was a young man from Tanzania who limped agonizingly toward the finish line.

Having been injured in a fall early in the race, his knees were bleeding, his leg muscles were cramping, and dehydration was setting in. Yet he kept on running. Finally, painfully, he crossed the finish line and fell to the ground. A reporter said to him: "You were injured early and you knew you couldn't win the race. Why didn't you just give up?"

He answered, "My country didn't send me five-thousand miles to start the marathon. They sent me here to finish the marathon." As he said that, I thought of the words of another man who had endured more difficulties than most of us can imagine—rejection, ridicule, shipwrecks, beatings, imprisonments. Yet, at the end of his life, as he awaited death in a Roman prison, the apostle Paul wrote to his young friend Timothy: "The time of my departure has come. I have fought the good fight, *I have finished the race, I have kept the faith*" (2 Timothy 4:6-7, emphasis added).

According to Dr. Harry Emerson Fosdick, many people are good starters but not good "stayers." When difficulties arise, they drop out of the race. Each time I attend a wedding I wonder if the bride and groom have enough staying power to get through disagreements, frustrations, and stresses such as 2:00 A.M. feedings, job loss, relocation, rebellious teenagers, and difficult in-laws.

Staying power is equally as important in the business world. There are necessary but boring aspects to every job, including volunteer positions. Beginning a new job, getting married, buying a new house or car, having a baby, and taking a vacation all begin with excitement and enthusiasm. Yet the intensity of these emotions eventually melts away, and when the road gets bumpy, many people are tempted to "bail out."

What gives us staying power? There are some simple strategies that can help us not to give up. One is to maintain an attitude of gratitude. Stay focused on what you appreciate rather than what you dislike. Likewise, learn to enjoy life rather than complain about it. Be the kind of person that others not only respect but also *enjoy* being around. Another is to set growth goals for yourself—in your job, marriage, parent-child relationships, home life, and so forth. Then, *don't give up!* And most important, live for something bigger than yourself—something that provides inner stability. For me, this is the Christian faith. Despite his difficulties, the apostle Paul could finish the race with joy and confidence because he was empowered by the presence of Christ.

Like Paul, we too can finish the race with God's help. Remember, strive for staying power, not just starting power!

Steps to Developing Staying Power

1. Determine that you will persevere, that you will "finish the race."
2. Remember that perseverance in the difficult times and places is possible only as we are empowered by the presence of Christ.
3. Maintain an attitude of gratitude. In the midst of vicissitudes, the apostle Paul could say, "Give thanks in all circumstances" (1 Thessalonians 5:18).
4. Set growth goals for yourself—in your job, your relationships, and your personal life.
5. Learn to enjoy life. Look for beauty in nature, in people, and in all evidences of God's faithfulness; look for challenges and possibilities in every problem; and look for opportunities to laugh daily.
6. Live for something bigger than you are: the purposes of God. This is made possible only as Christ

lives within you. Remember this paraphrase from Colossians 1:27: "The secret is this, [insert your name], Christ is alive in you bringing with him the hope of glorious things to come."

7. Recall and say aloud this biblical affirmation: "Be steadfast, immovable, always excelling in the work of the Lord, because you know that in the Lord your labor is not in vain" (1 Corinthians 15:58).

Chapter 9

Repair Any Spiritual Leakage

[Samson] did not know that the Lord had left him.

—Judges 16:20

W hat in the world has happened to you? You look wonderful. The last time I saw you, four years ago, I was sure you were ready to self-destruct. At the very least, you seemed likely to be putting your life slowly down the tubes." These were my opening words to a friend at a wedding reception.

Her reply was short, succinct, and very descriptive: "When I thought I was going down for the third time, I finally decided to take hold of one of the hooks God has offered me during these past eight hellish years."

"What was the hook?" I asked in anticipation of some spectacular miracle. Instead, my friend replied quietly, "Actually, the hook that literally saved my life consisted of two sentences in a book written by Dr. Alan Loy McGinnis, who is director of Valley Counseling Center in Glendale, California."

Though Dr. McGinnis is one of my favorite Christian authors, I wondered how two sentences could so dramatically change anyone's life. I especially wondered how they could effect a turnaround in someone whose life seemed on a collision course with disaster. My mind went back several years to the days when I first got to know her. I remembered how I met her when I was speaking before a group of teachers. At that particular meeting, she received an award for excellence in classroom teaching. She was intelligent, lively, highly motivated, and well respected by her colleagues.

Not long after she received the award, her house of life seemed to come tumbling down around her. Her husband announced that he was in love with another woman and wanted a divorce. She was both stunned and devastated. Worse than that, she falsely blamed herself for their marriage's failure and turned her anger and hurt inward upon herself. Not surprisingly, a cycle of depression began.

As often happens when one family member is dysfunctional, other members were affected. Some months after the divorce was final, one of her children began to take drugs. With this, my friend's emotional circuits became overloaded. Her depression deepened. She lost interest in her appearance. Though she once had been meticulous in her grooming, now she became almost slovenly. Her eating habits were unhealthy. To make matters worse, she began to drink excessively. She missed more and more days of work; and when she *was* in the classroom, she behaved like a zombie. Eventually she was fired.

Her close friends supported her, prayed for her, cared about her, confronted her, and even arranged for her to see a Christian counselor. But all this met with little success. These same friends also intervened on behalf of her child, who, after being in rehabilitation, is drug-free today. But my friend was a different story. When I last saw her, she seemed bent on self-destruction.

In her own words, she said that amid the misery of

her circumstances, there came a moment of truth for her. It happened on one "hungover" morning after several days of almost nonstop drinking. She looked in the mirror and really saw the woman she had become. From deep inside her came a voice that said: "You are going down for the third time." Every fiber of her being knew that it was true. It was then that she prayed her first truly honest prayer in years: "O God, I cannot keep myself from drowning; please help me."

She told me that when she walked down the hall to the living room, her eyes fell on a new book written by Dr. Alan Loy McGinnis, which had been given to her by a friend. She picked it up and read the words spoken by a college president to a student who, in despair over finances, had said that it was impossible for him to stay in college. The president had said: "Son, let's leave the impossible to God, and you and I will tackle the possible." That sentence, she said, stood out like a neon sign that read: "This is for you."

When she looked at the mess she had made of her life, the way out seemed impossible; but she decided to leave that to God. There were some "possibles" she could attack that very day. Two hours later, she was in her first meeting of Alcoholics Anonymous. It was there that she learned to live one day at a time. And it was there that, with the help of her supportive new friends, it became possible for her to work through her negative emotions.

The second life-changing sentence from Dr. McGinnis's book had an even greater power in her life. It was a quote from one of Dr. McGinnis's college professors: "Burnout comes most often from spiritual leakage." Suddenly, my friend knew that she had allowed her spirit to wither. At one time, Christ had been a constant companion, a source of spiritual energy. She realized that he had not moved; *she* had moved. At least, she had shifted her focus from her powerful resources and possibilities to her problems and her pain.

My friend learned to stop the spiritual leakage by recharging her spiritual batteries daily through Bible reading, meditation, and prayer. She returned to Sunday school and church. And she conditioned her mind with gratitude for her blessings.

Today she is a "new creation." It was God who used Dr. Alan Loy McGinnis to provide the hook she needed to keep her from going under. She is grateful to both, and all of her friends give thanks for a life that has been restored.

In our busy, fast-paced world, it is easy for spiritual power to leak silently and invisibly from our lives. Our spirits wither, and we become only the shells of what we were created to be. Emptiness, meaninglessness, and despair are the results. I challenge you to take time daily for spiritual disciplines—Bible reading, meditation, and prayer—and to take time each week to attend corporate worship so that the Living Water may enliven your parched spirit. Little by little, God's Spirit will flow through every facet of your being, empowering you for triumphant and abundant living.

Steps to Repairing Spiritual Leakage

1. Recognize that burnout and mild to serious depression can result from spiritual leakage, and remember that God offers "hooks" or helps to pull you out of your depression. These helps can come from a friend, a counselor, a book, a sermon, a circumstance, or somewhere else.
2. Stay spiritually "awake." Often we are like

Samson, who didn't know that the Lord—and his physical power—had left him (Judges 16:20). Warning signs for us may include emptiness, meaninglessness, or despair.

3. Take time daily for spiritual disciplines: Bible reading, meditation, and prayer.

4. Attend corporate worship weekly.

5. Believe that God's Spirit will refresh your parched spirit and empower you to live triumphantly.

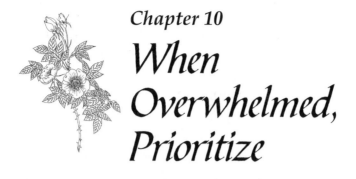

Chapter 10

When Overwhelmed, Prioritize

This one thing I do: forgetting what lies behind and straining forward to what lies ahead, I press on toward the goal for the prize of the heavenly call of God in Christ Jesus.

—Philippians 3:13-14

*I*t was a summer I'll never forget! In 1987, my husband and I ended a ministry of forty-six years. This emotional upheaval was accompanied by the necessity of tying up multitudinous "loose ends" before moving into our retirement home. Since our condominium was not ready when we needed to move out of the parsonage, we had to make two household moves in less than three months, with an interlude of living out of boxes. All of this left me feeling overwhelmed and fragmented.

As so often happens, God gave me the perfect solution to my dilemma through scripture. One morning as I read Philippians 3, the apostle Paul's words gave me a complete outline for what I needed to do. They are a great outline for everyone's daily living, for we all need a formula for finding calm in the storms of life and creating order out of chaos. He writes: "This *one* thing I do: forgetting what lies behind and straining forward to what lies ahead, I press on toward the goal for the prize of the heavenly call of God in Christ Jesus" (vv. 13-14, emphasis added).

First, Paul indicates that we need to choose the most important thing that needs doing without being distracted by all the lesser things that need doing. Later in the same week that God gave me these verses, I watched our five-year-old granddaughter work a picture puzzle that had over one hundred pieces. She did it in a room where her younger brother was watching cartoons on TV and several adults were talking and laughing. She concentrated fully on the puzzle and seemed oblivious to the distracting noises surrounding her. Through the years I have become more and more convinced that those who reach their daily and lifetime goals are the people who have the ability to see the important things that need to be done, to prioritize their activities, and then to do one thing at a time. This is the art of focused concentration, and it means we actually must plan to neglect other things—at least temporarily.

Second, Paul tells us to forget things that are past and to live in the twenty-four hours that today gives us. I wonder how much mental energy I've wasted in my lifetime "crying over spilt milk." It is a senseless waste of energy. While I believe we need to take time to analyze our mistakes and learn from them, we do not need to get bogged down in self-recriminations. Instead, we should plan how we will improve and then move on.

Third, Paul suggests that we *reach*. How often have you allowed yourself to dream creatively—to envision God's dream for you, your family, your company, your world? Thousands of people have never activated their gift of divine imagination. They simply do what comes next. Paul says that we need to reach for new challenges that will stretch our minds, skills, and habits.

Perhaps the most difficult word Paul uses is *press*. When athletes press against bars or lift weights, they are using every ounce of their strength. Maintaining

and building strength require work. A physical thera-
pist once told me that if we were to stay in bed for a
week, we would lose 75 percent of our muscle tone. It is
very easy to get "flabby"—physically, mentally, *and*
spiritually.

A few years ago I decided that I needed to use some
weights in my daily regimen of calisthenics. Since I have
a friend who is director of a women's fitness center, I
checked with her about the weights that would be safe
for a woman of my age and flabby physical condition.
For the first few weeks, I was so sore that I was tempted
to give up the endeavor and go back to comfortable flab-
biness. I decided, instead, to press on—to work at this
with determination and as much enthusiasm as I could
muster. Though I still have a long way to go, I can see
the improvement in muscle tone and stamina. Likewise,
in every area of the game of life, we must press on, using
every ounce of our energy, determination, and enthusiasm.

Finally, Paul says the prize is that we realize the heavenly call of God—or, in other words, the personal high
calling that God has for each of us. That is, we become,
through the help of Christ, all that we can be during our
pilgrimage here on planet Earth. Prayer and Bible study
play an important role in this process. In my own life, I
have found that realizing God's high calling is a lifelong
endeavor. Basically, as we come to know God's work
and experience the presence of Christ, we know ninety-
five percent of what this calling is: to love God with all
our hearts, souls, and minds, and to love our neighbors
as ourselves (Matthew 22:36-39). Determining the best
way to do this in particular situations requires careful
and prayerful thought. For the remaining five percent—
things such as unexpected opportunities or unexpected
changes or tragedies—we need to think clearly, pray

earnestly, and, at times, talk with a trusted friend or counselor.

Truly, this a good formula for living when we are feeling overwhelmed in everyday living!

Steps to Overcoming Feelings of Being Overwhelmed

Let Philippians 3:13-14 be your formula for creating order out of chaos:

1. *Focus* on the most important thing that needs to be done and allow yourself to neglect (temporarily) the less important things.
2. *Forget* things that are past and live in this twenty-four-hour time period.
3. *Reach* for the new challenges that will stretch your mind, skills, and habits.
4. Press toward your goals. In other words, "keep on keeping on," whether you feel like it or not.
5. Realize the personal high calling that God has for you through prayer, Bible study, and talking with a trusted friend or counselor.
6. Recall and say aloud Matthew 6:33 whenever you must prioritize: "But strive first for the kingdom of God and his righteousness, and all these things will be given to you as well."

Chapter 11

Keep Your Dreams Alive

I will pour out my spirit on all flesh; your sons and your daughters shall prophesy, your old men shall dream dreams, and your young men shall see visions.

—Joel 2:28

*I*n Jack Canfield and Mark Hansen's popular book *Chicken Soup for the Soul,* Dr. Ken Blanchard tells of his friends who brought their newborn son home from the hospital. Immediately upon their arrival, their four-year-old daughter, Sashi, insisted that they leave her alone in the room with her baby brother. When they asked why, she would give no reason. Though they had seen no indication that Sashi was jealous of her brother, they were hesitant to leave the baby alone in the room with her. Each time she mentioned this, they tried to distract her. One day, however, she was so insistent that they left the room, keeping the door ajar so that they could watch and hear. Putting her face close to her brother's, Sashi said, "Baby, tell me what God is like. I'm starting to forget."

In the secular society in which we live, it is easy to let the image of God dim in our consciousness, and thus in our lives. In January of 1996, I had an exciting reminder that God is alive and well and able to communicate his plans to those who will hear and heed. The occasion was the twenty-fifth anniversary of the Robert H. Schuller Institute for Successful Church Leadership in Garden Grove, California. I had been there in the early years of the Institute when my pastor husband took six of his staff members, encouraging us to stretch our minds and dream God's dream for our church. It was a transforming experience for my personal faith as well as my vision for the future. That year, 1977, there were between 300 and 400 persons in attendance. Today over 3,000 clergy and laypersons of many denominations from 10 countries come together each year to hear anew God's call and to learn new leadership skills.

The week-long twenty-fifth anniversary celebration began with a gala salute to Dr. and Mrs. Schuller for their vision in sponsoring the Institute. The Chancel of the vast Crystal Cathedral was aglow with colorful spring flowers banked by lush, green plants. The music, as varied as the messages, was magnificent and included a short concert by the Cathedral Choir under the direction of Frederick Swann, as well as contemporary music that included Dr. Schuller's favorite song, "The Impossible Dream."

An anniversary video included greetings and comments from persons who had built strong ministries as a result of the inspiration received at the Institute. Among them were David Yonggi Cho, pastor of the world's largest-membership church in Korea; Bill Hybels, pastor of Willow Creek Community Church in Chicago; and Walt Kallestead, pastor of Community Church of Joy in Glendale, Arizona.

As he responded to the accolades, Dr. Schuller told a little of the history of the Garden Grove Church, now known as the Crystal Cathedral. It began in 1955 with one member, his wife. When they found a few interested persons, they began meeting at the drive-in theater.

Today the Crystal Cathedral campus is one of the largest and most beautiful in the nation, and their ministries are worldwide in their outreach. One of the better-known ministries is the televised "Hour of Power" program seen in the United States, Europe, and Russia. The story of how it began, which Dr. Schuller told us that day, is a story about an exciting experiment in faith.

More than thirty years ago, the Reverend Dr. Billy Graham said to Dr. Schuller, "You ought to televise your worship service."

"That would be great," replied Dr. Schuller, "but how much would it cost?"

"Around $400,000," replied the evangelist.

"There is no way we can afford that," said the young pastor, who was struggling with church finances.

"Why don't you 'put out the fleece' and see if that's what God wants. That's what I did when I started my telecast and radio programs," said Dr. Graham.

Dr. Schuller, of course, knew the biblical story of Gideon putting out the fleece (see Judges 7:36-40), but he wasn't from a tradition that encouraged that kind of thing. Still, he was open to the idea. So Dr. Graham suggested that Dr. Schuller simply announce the following Sunday what he was considering and ask the members to fill out a pledge card that day. The "fleece" would be the one and only announcement; and if one half or more of the amount needed was pledged, they would go with the idea. If not, they would believe it was not in God's plan.

After church the following Sunday, the church administrator called Dr. Schuller and said, "Well, we have our answer. We received $198,000 in pledges." A relieved Dr. Schuller replied, "Good!" Then he called Dr. Graham, who counseled, "Wait until noon on Monday, since some people went home to talk over their pledges with their spouses." His prediction was accurate. By noon on Monday they were over the $200,000 mark!

Dr. Schuller gave permission for lights to be installed on the arboretum where they were meeting for worship. In the middle of the installation, he received a call indicating that they would have to install another transformer and would have to pay for it—$10,000 in cash, which would have to be paid by the end of the following day.

Pausing to look at the large audience, Dr. Schuller said, "We had less than $4,000 in our church budget, and I certainly didn't have the money personally. So, I prayed: 'God, if you want this to happen, please provide the way.'"

The next day, Dr. Schuller went through his scheduled appointments. At 3:00 p.m. he had an appointment with a couple he did not know. When they came in, he assumed they were there for marriage counseling, so he asked, "What's your problem?"

"No problem," they said with a smile. We were in your church last November, and you preached on tithing. That day we decided to try it. Today we want to give you our first quarter's tithe to use where it is needed." It was a check for exactly $10,000. The "Hour of Power" telecast was launched.

Dr. Schuller's visionary ministry has been undergirded at every step by prayer and obedience. His vision of the God whom Jesus revealed has never faded. As a result of his powerful testimony, all of us in attendance at the Institute had our own vision sharpened and redefined. His story inspired us not only to dare to dream but to keep our dreams alive.

How do we begin? Like Dr. Schuller, I have learned through experience that a dream has to be crafted carefully and prayerfully and then tested (see step 3 below).

Next we must count the cost of the dream in time, money, preparation, and planning—and be willing to pay the price. We keep the dream alive by reading the inspirational stories of people, such as Dr. Schuller, who have fulfilled their dreams despite major setbacks. Most of all, we keep the dream alive through faith and prayer. Then we give God the glory.

Go ahead. Dare to dream, and then keep your dreams alive!

Steps to Keeping Your Dreams Alive

1. Recognize that you don't have to stay the way you are! God is constantly stretching you and calling you into the future.

2. Determine that you will not settle into ruts—even comfortable ruts. Train yourself to see possibilities in every facet of your life—in your family, job, church, community, and relationships. Possibilities can become dreams—God's dreams. Don't be afraid if a dream seems too big.

3. "Test" your dream with two questions: Is there anything in this dream that is not in keeping with the will of God, according to Christ? Is there anything in this dream that will hurt me or anyone else? If it passes both questions and continues to excite you, go for it!

4. Be sure to count the cost of your dream. Jesus said: "For which of you, intending to build a tower, does not first sit down and estimate the cost, to see whether he has enough to complete it?" (Luke 14:28). The cost of a dream usually includes time, money,

preparation (sometimes including additional education), and careful planning.

5. Pray for God's guidance, for courage, and for obedience.

6. When the doors open, walk through them in confidence.

7. Hold on to your dream, despite setbacks and negative reactions.

8. Be sure to give God thanks as your dream develops.

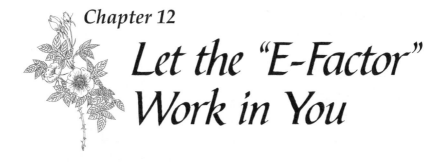

Chapter 12

Let the "E-Factor" Work in You

"These people who have been turning the world upside down have come here also."

—Acts 17:6

*H*e exuded energy, enthusiasm, and vitality. I was impressed by his aliveness. In fact, meeting and talking with him made me feel as if I had just received a B-12 shot!"

These were the words I used to tell my husband about my first impression of Joe, business consultant and interim president of a services company. Through employees of the company, I had heard of Joe's leadership and relational skills and, most especially, of his ability to motivate others. As I met with him that day, I learned firsthand that, without a doubt, Joe embodies the "E-Factor"—an important quality being stressed by more and more businesses today.

The "E-Factor" is not included in the list of job skills traditionally sought in an employee—things such as knowledge of economics, accounting, marketing, or computer technology. Rather, it is an invisible factor— the results of which are quite evident. Basically, the "E-Factor" is sustained enthusiasm. This kind of enthusiasm is not back-slapping, phony exuberance or loud laughter. Rather, those who posses it are self-motivated and energetic, work well with others, and create a climate of excitement and expectation. Such individuals generally are outgoing, though some more introspective persons exhibit the "E-Factor" in their quiet strength. Most people who have studied enthusiasm agree on two things: It is a skill that can be acquired, and it makes a vast difference in one's life. As Ralph Waldo Emerson wrote, "Nothing great is ever achieved without enthusiasm." To be sure, we all should remember Henry David Thoreau's warning: "None are so old as those who have outlived enthusiasm."

Exactly what is enthusiasm, and how do we acquire it? The famous English historian Arnold Toynbee once wrote, "Apathy can only be overcome by enthusiasm and enthusiasm can only be aroused by two things; first, an ideal that takes the imagination by storm; and second, a definite, intelligible plan for putting that ideal into practice" (quoted in Norman Vincent Peale's booklet entitled *Enthusiasm*). Most observers agree enthusiasm is a dynamic quality that brings the personality alive, releasing dormant powers. Actually, the word *enthusiasm* comes from two Greek words: *en theos*, meaning "God within." I am convinced that when we truly believe in God and seek to live in his purposes, we are empowered to do more than we believe possible. Jesus said, "All things can be done for the one who believes" (Mark 9:23).

In his booklet on enthusiasm, Dr. Norman Vincent Peale suggests some practical helps for becoming more enthusiastic, such as

- stay sensitized to the thrill of living;
- hold the image of an enthusiastic you in your consciousness;

- act as if you had enthusiasm;
- start each day with enthusiastic thoughts;
- put vitality-activating quotations and Bible passages into your mind to spur enthusiasm;
- and love life and people.

In my own life, I have learned that negative emotions and enthusiasm don't mix. Optimism is an essential ingredient for enthusiasm. According to Dr. Martin Seligman, optimism and negativism are learned responses, usually taught to us by our primary caregiver in the early years of life. Thereafter, we tend to repeat our "mental tapes" over and over through the years unless we make a disciplined effort to interrupt the cycle. Three things have helped me to change a very negative pattern I developed early in my life: (1) consciously changing my thoughts; (2) wearing a rubber band which I pop against my wrist when I say or think something negative; (3) and, most important, using positive biblical affirmations to reprogram my thinking. Laughter also seems to kindle enthusiasm in me, as does a sincere interest in other people. When we help and encourage others, our own power of optimism is further released. This is true in business as well as in personal life. I once heard Tom Peters say that if he were trying to choose between two prospective employees of fairly equal ability, he would choose the enthusiastic one because that person could motivate himself or herself and others.

Finally, enthusiasm keeps us strong for daily living. Once while reading about a brass foundry, I discovered a wonderful analogy between the molten brass and people. When the brass is heated in a crucible to a temperature of 2,200 degrees Fahrenheit, it becomes very strong. In fact, it cannot be broken. On the other hand, when it is cold, it is very brittle. In a way, we are like the molten brass in those crucibles. When we are surcharged with spiritual fire and enthusiasm, nothing can break us. But if we let the spiritual fire and enthusiasm die down, even the small blows of circumstance can crack and shatter us. So let's keep the "E-Factor" operative in us!

Steps to Developing the E-Factor

1. Believe with Emerson that "nothing great is ever achieved without enthusiasm." Believe in God and seek to live in God's purposes. Remember that enthusiasm comes from two Greek words: *en theos*, meaning "God within."
2. Believe with Jesus that "all things can be done for the one who believes" (Mark 9:23).
3. Stand guard over your thoughts and eliminate the negative, stressful, fear-ridden thoughts. Remember, *you* are in control of your thoughts!
4. Interrupt your negative thoughts and replace them with positive affirmations. Begin by looking carefully at the old "scripts" you are playing in your mind. For example, my mother was a pessimist and a worrier. She habitually said things such as, "This is the worst day of my life"; "I've never been so rushed"; and "I'm under terrible stress." Through habit, I was replaying those tapes, thus making myself negative, unhappy, and over-stressed. I had to interrupt the cycle.
5. Reprogram your thoughts through biblical affirmations such as Philippians 4:13: "I can do all things through [Christ] who strengthens me."

6. Learn to love life and people, to laugh, and to look for the beautiful things in life.

7. Stay in close touch with Christ, the Master of joy. In my experience, nothing spurs enthusiasm more than the inspiration that comes from this one relationship!

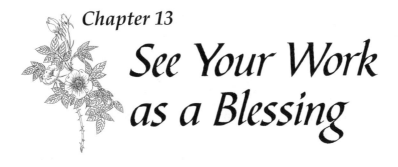

Chapter 13

See Your Work as a Blessing

Let the favor of the Lord our God be upon us, and prosper for us the work of our hands.

—Psalm 90:17

---

*H*is eyes looked hollow; the expression on his face seemed wooden; his voice lacked enthusiasm; even his walk was lethargic. What a surprise! Through the years, this man had appeared confident, energetic, enthusiastic, and competent. As I talked with him, I discovered the reason for the change. At age fifty-two, he had lost his job, an executive position with a large corporation.

He lost his job, not because he had done anything wrong or because he was ineffective. Instead, he was a victim of a corporate takeover. For weeks he had sought, without success, a comparable position. He even had been turned down for the lesser positions for which he had applied because he was overqualified. The disappointment and despair he felt were evident in his physical appearance. I knew this man to be more aware than most of the privilege of work.

When I thought of his situation, I remembered something foolish I said when I was twenty and a college student. Reacting to the pressures of midterm exams and the quickly approaching deadlines for papers, I had immaturely exclaimed, "If I were rich, I would never work again!" Of all the dumb things I have said in my lifetime, that was one of the dumbest. We were not created to be sedentary, but to be creative and productive people.

How often many of us either take our work for granted or don't consider it a blessing. I remember a particular visit I had several years ago with my sister, who was in a nursing home and unable to articulate many of her thoughts and feelings. That day I found her badly nauseated and in unrelenting pain. She, who has been one of the most productive persons I have ever known—a teacher, a school principal, and a county supervisor of elementary education—is now confined almost entirely to her bed because of rheumatoid arthritis and lupus. When I mentioned that I had a heavy schedule for September, she replied, "Be very grateful that you are healthy enough to keep it."

My sister was right. The ability to use our time and talents in productive work is one of life's greatest blessings. It was the Greek philosopher Aristotle who long ago taught that "happiness comes chiefly by some productive act, a working in the way of excellence." He said that our happiest moments are not those in which we ask how to be happy, but those in which we so lose ourselves in some creative task that we forget to take our emotional pulse.

Sometimes I wonder if the reason so many of us run away from life or seek only tension-relieving activities rather than achievement-oriented activities or become content with mediocrity in the workplace is that we no longer view our work as a vocation. Having a *vocation* means that we see our work not only as a job but also as an investment of ourselves—our God-given talents, time, energy, and creativity—in something that will make a difference for good in the world. It is a way of seeing work as a window through which the divine light can shine in a special way.

The late Earl Nightingale, who was considered by many business and professional people as the dean of personal development, told the story of a young friend of his who sought passage to the Orient on a freighter. The ship looked worn and ill kept. The staterooms were far from the luxurious ones his friend had seen on the QE II, or even on ordinary ships. In fact, the entire ship looked as if nobody cared about what happened to it.

That is, no one seemed to care until he entered the engine room. The young man had never seen a more immaculate room. It was a "spit and polish"-looking place from top to bottom. There was no doubt that someone cared about it and worked to keep it clean. He expressed his delight to the engineer and asked how it could be so clean when the rest of the ship was so grimy. The old engineer, with a look of triumph, replied, "I got the glory in my soul about this engine room."

If all of us could see the glory in whatever job is ours, what a different world we would have. We would not need constant reminders to seek excellence. No matter how trivial the task, if we could do it to the best of our ability and do it as an offering to God, we could restore dignity to the workplace.

There is a story about three men who were laying brick for an English cathedral. Someone asked each of them separately what he was doing. One replied, "I am working for two dollars an hour." Another replied, "I'm laying brick." The third answered, "I'm building a cathedral."

If teachers, parents, electricians, factory workers, and business and professional people could perceive their jobs as something that can make a difference, that perception would bless their lives as well as ennoble our nation and our world. William James was right when he said, "The great use of life is to spend it for something that will outlast it."

As we face life, even on difficult days, may it be said of us what was said of an Englishman during the Cromwellian turmoil. These words are inscribed in a chapel at Stanton Harold near the heart of England: "In the year 1663, when all things sacred were, throughout the nation, either demolished or profaned, Sir Robert Shirley Baronet founded this church; whose singular praise it is to have done the best things in the worst times."

Steps to Seeing Your Work as a Blessing

1. Believe that life is an incredible gift from God. I love this saying: "Yesterday is history; tomorrow is a mystery; today is a gift. That's why we call it the present."
2. Remember that because life is a gift from God, what you do with it is your gift to God.
3. Remember that we were created to be creative and productive people, not sedentary creatures.
4. Whether you are a paid employee or a volunteer, continue to see your work as the creative use of your God-given talents, time, energy, and personality.
5. Do your work to the glory of God, and you will do it with excellence and joy. When you do this, your work will bless others.
6. However seemingly insignificant your work sometimes may be, always remember that you are "building a cathedral."

Chapter 14

Know How to Be "Real"

He who began a good work in you will bring it to completion.

—Philippians 1:6 (RSV)

Hugh Walpole wrote a delightful story entitled "The Three Princes of Serendip." It describes not only a journey of the princes but also the unexpected incidents or surprises that occur along the way. These are called serendipities.

I have discovered many serendipities on my journey as a grandmother. One of them is the excitement of rediscovering some of the stories and books I loved as a child. When our grandchildren were in elementary school, we took them to the community theater to see *The Velveteen Rabbit*. The circular youth theater was packed with pre-school and elementary-aged children along with their parents and grandparents. It was almost as much fun to watch the faces of the children as to watch the performance.

The play, adapted from the story by Margery Williams, is an enchanting tale of how a stuffed animal, a velveteen rabbit, becomes real when he is deeply loved by a four-year-old girl named Samantha. A part of the dialogue that has stayed with me through the years is when the rabbit says to the Skin Horse, "Does it hurt to be real?" The answer: "Sometimes it does. You begin to feel with another person, and sometimes that hurts." "Well," continues the rabbit, "do you become real all at once?" "No," says the Skin Horse, "it happens a little at a time. You *become*."

In a world that seems plagued with phoniness—where scams are reported almost daily by the press; where fraud is evidenced on a national and international scale; and where many individuals are encouraged to pretend to be what they are not—most of us yearn to be "real." We want to be people of integrity. We want our dreams and our deeds to be one. We want our actions to square with our words. Perhaps we need to remember that the Skin Horse said we don't become real all at once. We become.

After a man and woman have said their marriage vows during a wedding ceremony, we say they are married. Obviously, they are not married until they go through the ceremony, but we know that the ceremony is only the first step of the journey. A happy marriage is hammered out on the anvil of joy and sorrow, pain and pleasure, work and play, laughter and tears. The married couple are "becoming."

We also say that the same couple are parents when their first child is born. Yet anyone who has reared a child to adulthood knows that physical birth is only the tiniest beginning of parenthood. They are becoming real parents as, through the years, they love, guide, educate, listen to, discipline, and pray for that child. Parenthood is not a *fait accompli*.

When I made a profession of my faith in Christ, I became a Christian. Yet that was only the beginning. In a deeper sense, I am becoming a Christian daily as I continue to grow spiritually. This scripture verse in

Philippians always encourages me when I feel that my progress is slow: "He who began a good work in you will bring it to completion" (1:6 RSV). As a reminder of this, I keep a small, framed statement on my desk that reads: "Be patient with me. God hasn't finished with me yet. I am a Christian under construction."

To become real—to become persons of integrity in a world that often seems to honor duplicity—we need to do several things. First, we need to live intentionally. It is so easy to put our lives on "automatic pilot" and to do what comes next rather than live intentionally out of our highest values. We may be busy and efficient coasting through life, but we likely will not be very effective. In a seminar I attended several years ago, business and management consultant Peter Drucker said, "Management is doing things right; leadership is doing the right things." Likewise, I once heard Dr. Stephen Covey advise that efficient management without effective leadership is like straightening the deck chairs on the *Titanic*.

Second, we need to remember that, as individuals, we are responsible for our lives. In 1965, I read Dr. Viktor Frankl's marvelous book *Man's Search for Meaning*. Perhaps only then did I fully understand our wonderful God-given freedom of choice. Actually, we *choose* the kind of persons we are. Dr. Frankl, a Viennese psychiatrist, was imprisoned in the death camps of Nazi Germany and experienced torture and unimaginable indignities. In addition, his parents, brother, and wife either died in those camps or were sent to gas ovens. In the midst of that terrible inhumanity, Viktor Frankl discovered what he called the last of the human freedoms— the freedom to decide how circumstances were going to affect him. Like Dr. Frankl, we can't always choose what will happen to us, but we always can choose our reactions.

Yes, as the Skin Horse said to the Velveteen Rabbit, sometimes it does hurt to be real. But only then can we live with love, joy, peace of mind, and freedom.

Steps to Becoming "Real"

1. Remember that being "real" doesn't happen all at once. You *become* through daily decisions and actions.
2. Live intentionally out of your highest values.
3. Don't play the blame game. Take responsibility for your life.
4. Never forget this good news: You are not alone in this attempt. Claim the promise of Philippians 1:6.
5. Remember that only when your deeds square with your words can you live with love, joy, peace, and freedom.

Chapter 15

Choose Life and Live Abundantly

I call heaven and earth to witness against you today that I have set before you life and death, blessings and curses. Choose life . . .

—Deuteronomy 30:19

As we stand on the edge of this new century and new millennium, what equipment do we need? I think it is important to consider seriously what we *most* need. Let me suggest four characteristics: (1) aliveness, (2) purpose, (3) discipline, and (4) joy.

First, we need the characteristic of aliveness. In his poem "The Road Not Taken," Robert Frost speaks of two roads diverging in a yellow wood and ends with these two lines: "I took the one less traveled by, and that has made all the difference." It has been my observation that the people who are making a difference and are living with vitality have chosen "the road less traveled." Jesus called this the narrow road (Matthew 7:14 NIV). He also said, "I came that [you] may have life, and have it abundantly" (John 10:10). Centuries before, God spoke through Moses to the children of Israel in the wilderness and said, "I call heaven and earth to witness against you today that I have set before you life and death, blessings and curses. Choose life . . ." (Deuteronomy 30:19).

The first step on the road to continued aliveness is

made by our choice. It is so easy to fall into habits that lead to ruts. Aliveness demands that we understand life is a gift, a precious gift, and that we must become resolute in doing whatever is necessary not to miss this one chance we have to live it fully! When *Time* magazine chose Pope John Paul II, a religious figure, as the 1994 Man of the Year, they did so because, they said, "in a time of moral confusion, he is *resolute* about his ideals" (emphasis added). You see, how we live our lives is a *choice.* Let us choose aliveness.

After choosing aliveness, our next step is to determine our purpose in life. Leonardo da Vinci was once asked, "When is a painting finished?" He replied, "When it fulfills the intent of the artist." In like manner, a life is complete when it fulfills the intent of the creator. This necessitates our asking questions such as "Why am I here?"; "What are my special gifts and talents?"; "In my best moments, what do I most want to do with these abilities?"; and "Are my desires in keeping with God's purposes?" Remember that we are building for eternity, not just for a short earthly life. Dr. Leonard Sweet, Dean of Drew University Theological School, said it so well in his monthly publication *Sweet's Soul Café*: "It is important that each of us live soul-fully—to grow and garden a vital, vibrant, healthy soul, and to face the problems of life not only with our minds but also with our souls."

To be fully alive, we also need discipline. Most of us constantly feel the need of disciplining our bodies—eating less junk food and following a regular program of exercise. The secret of good results is not how well we start, but how disciplined we are in following our regime. So it is with purpose. We must set goals, and we must stay with them! We can't be couch potatoes, half-hearted about the things that are so important: faith, family, work, friends, recreation, and social involvement in things that will make a difference. We have to be persistent and discipline ourselves to follow through on our purposeful goals.

Dr. Viktor Frankl, the noted Viennese psychiatrist who spent years in a concentration camp in Germany, wrote in his book *Man's Search for Meaning*: "It is far more dangerous not to set goals than not to reach your goals." In many of his speeches following his liberation, he emphasized the importance of setting goals. He indicated that a goal helps you to bring the future into the present and gives you something toward which to strive. Then he used the example of Moses and the children of Israel being led through the wilderness by a pillar of cloud by day and a pillar of fire by night. He explained that although we can't catch up with a cloud or with fire, they, like goals, keep us moving in the right direction. I'm convinced that when we get close to reaching our goals, we need to dream again and set new ones. Otherwise, we get bogged down in what "is" rather than what "can be."

Finally, all of us need to recapture joy in our lives. Recently I heard speaker Robert Stuberg say that we are a society of people who are striving harder and harder for more and more things, yet we are enjoying them less and less. He said that we are living on the surface of life while the real person—the spirit—is wilting and dying within.

Joy, as you know, is not the same as happiness. Happiness comes from the root word *happenstance*, meaning "to happen." Happiness comes when good things happen to us, such as a promotion, a scholarship for college, marriage, the birth of a child, a new house or car, the opportunity to travel, and so forth. Joy, on the other hand, is a fruit of the Spirit, as the apostle Paul explains in Galatians 5:22. It is the sure knowledge that nothing can happen in life that God and we can't handle together, because we are empowered by the Holy Spirit. Even in the midst of pain and difficulties, there is something that sings inside us when we allow God's Spirit to live within.

Joy comes as we live out of gratitude for life and all the opportunities we have to live it fully. We come to see that possessions are not nearly as important as relationships—with God, with ourselves, and with others. It is only when we cultivate this inward joy that we are fully able to enjoy the ebb and flow of daily living. Only then do we take time to "smell the flowers"—to see beauty all around us. In his publication *Sweet's Soul Café,* Dr. Leonard Sweet reminds us that if we are to be vibrantly alive, we must remember this: "Nothing you and I do is more important in life than to grow a soul. Soul is the essence of who we are, the character of our being, the truth of our spirit."

So, we stand on the edge of tomorrow with growing excitement and expectation! The Phillips translation of Romans 8:19 says this in a unique way: "The whole creation is on tiptoe to see the wonderful sight of the sons [and daughters] of God coming into their own." Let us choose life!

 Steps to Choosing Life and Living Abundantly

1. Exercise the gift of choice. Even in the midst of circumstances over which you have little or no control, you can choose your reactions.

2. Determine your purpose in life. As a Christian, remember that you are created in the image of God (Genesis 1:27), redeemed by Jesus Christ (John 3:16), and empowered by the Holy Spirit (John 1:12).

3. Practice discipline. Begin by setting goals: (1) physical goals, such as eating nutritionally, exercising regularly, getting adequate sleep, and learning to handle stress; (2) mental goals, such as continuing to grow by taking classes, reading, listening to tapes, and observing and learning from others; and (3) spiritual goals, such as worshiping God privately and publicly, reading God's Word, and praying.

4. Recapture joy. It is as Paul writes in Galatians 5:22-23: Joy is the fruit of Christ's Spirit living within us.

5. Move into the new millennium with excitement and expectation!

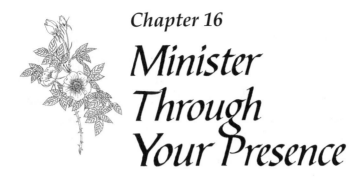

Chapter 16

Minister Through Your Presence

Comfort, O comfort my people, says your God. Speak tenderly.

—Isaiah 40:1-2

*A*s a college student, I had two criteria for whether or not a movie was good: if it made me laugh, or if it made me cry. Though I have added a few additional requisites through the years, I still like to be moved emotionally by a film. According to these criteria, the movie *Shadowlands*, which was released several years ago, was excellent, though I should have taken more tissues!

My husband and I have little time in our lives for recreation, so we choose the few movies we see carefully. Yet because we both have been influenced by the writings of C. S. Lewis, we knew that *Shadowlands* was a must.

During my freshman year in college, I went through a period of honest doubt about my Christian faith. The course "Religion 101" raised some mind-boggling questions and made me feel, at times, as if the rug had been pulled out from under me. In retrospect, I realize that my mind needed stretching. My beliefs had never been tested. They were neatly filed in my mind, but they were provincial and narrow. My God was too small.

Yet the stretching process was painful. I resisted all simplistic answers and felt that most Christians with whom I came in contact never used their minds when it came to their belief systems. Then a college friend gave me the book *Mere Christianity*, by C. S. Lewis, which she herself had just discovered. As I read it, I felt as if I had come home to faith, but to a much larger and more challenging one. I found myself in the presence of a brilliant scholar who answered each of my questions so clearly and logically that all my intellectual pride melted away. I had been at a crossroads, and that book, plus Lewis's *The Screwtape Letters*, pointed me back to genuine faith.

Through the years I have watched with amazement as Lewis's books continue to inspire, challenge, and confront people of all ages. In the last church where my husband served as pastor, it was exciting to see a young engineer lead summer studies for middle school students on *The Chronicles of Narnia*, a series of books by C. S. Lewis. He had a way of making the studies dramatically realistic and exciting, and the young people loved them. In that same church, the youth director always used *Mere Christianity* with high school seniors for six months before they went away to college. Her intent was to enable them to clarify their beliefs and stand firm against all the vicissitudes of college life.

The movie *Shadowlands* is based on a little-known period in the life of Lewis when he was a professor of classics at Oxford University. After showing a glimpse of the sedate life of the Oxford don in 1952, the movie moves quickly to the arrival of an admiring pen pal from America—Joy Gresham, played by Debra Winger. She and her son turn the quiet, emotionally guarded life of Lewis upside down.

Lewis and Gresham both converted to Christianity after spending many years as atheists. Beyond that, they are totally different. She is fearlessly honest and adventuresome; she is a poet, a divorced woman, and a parent. Lewis, played by Anthony Hopkins, was deeply hurt as a child by his mother's death and consequently has shied away as an adult from both women and children. It is a mystery to his colleagues at Oxford how he can write bestsellers for the young when he doesn't know any children himself.

Though I won't outline the entire plot, I will say it is a beautiful film—with beautiful English scenery, beautiful music performed by the London Symphony Orchestra, and a beautifully tender, though sad, love story.

Shadowlands shows us people with profound pain and profound faith. It affirms the goodness of God in the face of unfair suffering, and it testifies that love is worth the hurt it brings. For me, one of the most poignant scenes is when Lewis, who usually is extremely articulate, feels he has no consolation to offer his stepson, Douglas. He discovers that what they really need is to cry together. How often we are perplexed about what to say to someone who has suffered a terrible loss. That scene reminds us that we don't have to say anything. There is a ministry of presence, and it is powerful. We simply have to "be there" for our friends.

Shadowlands reveals another truth: While few make it through life without pain, there is always reason to press on. At one point in the film, Joy Gresham makes this wry comment: "The pain then [in separation by death] is a part of the happiness now."

In a day when sleaze and scandal are a part of every newscast and many movies, it is wonderfully refreshing to see a true story of eternal values—love, honor, hope, and faith—portrayed so sensitively. Even if you've already seen *Shadowlands*, give yourself a present and rent the video when you have the opportunity. And always remember this: There is a ministry of presence. Use this ministry with others who are experiencing pain, disappointment, and loss.

Steps to Ministering Through Your Presence

1. One of the best ways to make caring for others a true ministry is to be sure that your faith in Christ is strong and vital.
2. Don't be afraid of honest doubt. It is through our doubts that we are motivated to speak the truth. After all, all truth is God's truth. Don't try to put God in too narrow a mold. Remember, Jesus told us to "search, and you will find" (Matthew 7:7).
3. Read the Bible and other inspirational books. Look for books whose authors struggled to find a strong faith and emerged victorious (for example, *Mere Christianity,* by C. S. Lewis).
4. Put your faith into action by being present with friends who are experiencing difficulty or tragedy.
5. Remember that the ministry of presence is powerful. You don't need to have all the answers. In fact, you don't have to say anything at all. Others will know that you care enough to be with them.

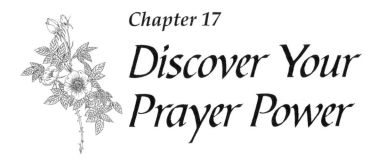

Chapter 17

Discover Your Prayer Power

The prayer of the righteous is powerful and effective.

—*James 5:16*

---

*I*t happened in the mid-1980s in one of the remote provinces of China. For the first time since the Communists had come into power, a Christian relief organization had been invited to help China in the wake of a devastating flood. It was a great opportunity, and World Vision responded quickly and joyfully. Finally, the relief work was completed, and the Communist Chief of the province invited the American Chair of World Vision, Dr. Roberta Hestenes, for a twenty-one-day inspection tour.

While telling the story during her C. S. Lewis lecture at the University of Tennessee at Chattanooga, Dr. Hestenes said that by the eighteenth day of the tour, she was fatigued and homesick. Every minute of every day had been scheduled, and for most of those long days, she had traveled in a caravan of jeeps up and down treacherous mountains and into the interior of the province. The eighteenth day was Sunday, and as they jostled along roads that were little more than trails, an unspoken prayer welled up in her heart: "Lord, it's

Sunday, and I am lonely. Back home, my family and friends are going to church to glorify your name. I miss my family, and I miss worship. In this openly atheistic country, if there is any way you can let me meet another Christian today, I will be most grateful. Amen."

At their first stop that morning, the Communist Chief, who had accompanied her each day, approached her, saying through an interpreter, "I am sorry. I am really sorry."

"Sorry about what?" she asked curiously.

"I am sorry that we have a free hour. I thought I had planned well, but they won't be ready for us at the next stop for another hour."

An exhausted Dr. Hestenes reported that she felt like saying, "Hallelujah! Let's be quiet and rest." But her host was asking, "Is there anything you'd like to do during these sixty minutes?"

Suddenly, Dr. Hestenes remembered that just a little distance back, she had seen what she thought was a church as they bounced along the mountainous road. "I saw a church a few miles back, and I'd like to visit it."

"We have no churches," her Communist host replied curtly.

In a conciliatory manner she said, "Maybe my eyes deceived me." Before she could go on, he replied, "Your eyes deceived you."

Remembering her prayer of the morning, Dr. Hestenes kindly but firmly persisted: "Just in case they didn't, could we take a look? After all, we have a free hour." Reluctantly, the Communist leader agreed.

As they turned their vehicles around, Roberta prayed earnestly, "Please let me see that cross again." The caravan had traveled less than two miles when she shouted, "Stop!" In the distance, the white cross was gleaming. While the Communists got out of the Jeeps for a smoke,

Dr. Hestenes and the interpreter began walking through overgrown brush in the direction of the church. She gasped as she looked upon a small but beautiful Christian church located, it seemed, in the middle of nowhere. A young woman deacon greeted them warmly and told them that the pastor was treating someone in the clinic but would be with them shortly. The church service would not begin until everyone completed their day's work.

"How many people attend your services?" asked Dr. Hestenes. Expecting to hear that there were between five and ten persons, she was stunned by the deacon's reply: "On a bad day we have about five hundred." There, in a remote section of an atheistic country, the Christian church was flourishing. The banner at the front of the church displayed John 3:16 in Chinese.

The pastor appeared shortly and told Dr. Hestenes that for eighteen years their congregation had prayed that a Christian from a free country would come to visit them, and that she was the answer to their prayers. When the short visit ended, those three Christians held hands as the pastor thanked God for his faithfulness in hearing and answering their prayers. Dr. Hestenes reported that there were tears running down the cheeks of the usually composed Chinese faces, as well as her own.

As I heard that story, I thought of Dr. Frank Laubach, widely known for his leadership in a worldwide literacy movement. His book *Prayer, the Mightiest Force in the World* has influenced the prayer lives of millions around the world, including my own. He says that there is no right or wrong way to pray. Rather, we need to remember that prayer is based on a relationship between us and God and is the communication that results from that relationship.

Dr. Laubach reminds us that in a good relationship between two people—whether it be a marriage, friendship, or parent-child relationship—the communication channels always remain open. There are structured times when we talk and listen to each other, and there are times when we are apart and focus on other endeavors. Yet even in those times when we are apart, we still are open to any call that may come from our loved one. This, he says, is the way it should be in our relationship with God. We need structured time to talk and listen to God, but we should keep the channels open at all times. Dr. Laubach suggests that throughout each day we use what he calls "shooting prayers." For example, when we think of a friend or a troubled stranger, we shoot a prayer in that person's direction. We can do this when we are sitting in heavy traffic, participating in a business meeting, having a conversation with a child, riding on an airplane, or whatever we may be doing. His book is full of illustrations about how God's power and love flow through us to others.

Days before that memorable Sunday in China, Dr. Hestenes had been shooting prayers of good will toward her Communist host. Perhaps it was that very release of spiritual power that God used to answer both her cry of loneliness and the prayers of a faithful congregation in an atheistic culture. Prayer is indeed powerful!

Steps to Discovering Your Prayer Power

1. First, understand what prayer is. According to Dr. Frank Laubach in his book *Prayer, the Mightiest Force in the World,* prayer is

based on a relationship between us and God and is the communication that results from that relationship.

2. Remember that prayer is vitally important to every disciple of Jesus Christ. The one thing the disciples asked Jesus to teach them was how to pray (see Luke 11:1). These were religious Jews who prayed several times daily, yet they wanted the prayer experience of Jesus, who came out of his prayer time energized, empowered, and marked by a radiant countenance.

3. Spend time alone with God in prayer. Just as we spend time with those we love—talking, listening, expressing appreciation, telling about our problems and our joys, making requests—so also we should spend time with God, sharing and listening.

4. Have a time for structured prayer, but always keep the channels of communication open. For example, in the morning, ask, "Lord, what are we going to do today?" Then, throughout the day, look and listen for "nudges"—times when you can share God's love with others.

5. Use "shooting prayers." When you think of a friend or troubled stranger, shoot a prayer in that person's direction.

6. Start the day with a prayer, and close the day by turning over to God any problems and concerns—perhaps as you remove each item of clothing. Then thank God for his presence and rest in his loving care.

Chapter 18

Try Giving Yourself Away

"It is more blessed to give than to receive."

—Acts 20:35

I was moved to tears when I read an account of compassion experienced and expressed by a church youth group making a missions trip to Jamaica. It was written by my granddaughter, Ellen, age sixteen, and I have her permission to include it here. The assignment, given in a sophomore English class, was to "look at a photograph and write your feelings and thoughts about it." The picture Ellen chose was of her friend Ansley sitting on the bedside of a sick and elderly man in a Jamaican infirmary. The essay she wrote in response, which follows, caused me to realize anew the importance of intangible gifts such as love, compassion, time, encouragement, generosity, and hope.

"Infirmary," by Ellen Mohney

By looking superficially at this picture, you cannot see or begin to understand why it *fills* me with a deep longing to be in that place once again, and why sometimes it brings tears to my eyes. You may see my friend in this picture, playing the role of short-term missionary, holding the hand of an old Jamaican man who is covered by blue and white striped sheets. You may notice the concrete wall in the background or the small chest with a cup, crackers, some personal products, and an old, worn book on top of it.

But what you don't see are the things I see most. You don't see the flies on the man's face, the urine splattered over the floor, or the family of wild pigs just outside the door. You don't see the thirty other men who will share this one room for the rest of their lives, or the blind man in perfectly good health, whose family left him on the doorstep of the infirmary because they were tired of watching out for him. You don't see the man in the back room with rotted-out teeth and huge sores on his feet as he urges me to "praise da Lord"; the young man, no older than twenty-five, abandoned by his family because he was mentally retarded; the hurt and loneliness in the men's eyes as each of them realizes that their children are not coming to visit them on their day—Father's Day.

When I look at this picture, I see, smell, and feel all that went on that day. I see my friend, teammate, and "big sister" sitting not quite comfortably on the side of a bed as she tightly holds the hand of a man whom she has just fallen in love with and who has changed her heart and perspective on life forever. I see twenty-five white youths being stretched farther than they have been before as each roams between the cots of the men—their cheeks wet with tears. I see one of my best friends slowly walking through the hot, muggy room, strumming her guitar and singing as a few youth follow close behind, and the excitement and joy of watching the man's eyes when they agreed to sing his favorite song, "Amazing Grace." I see one of my friends reading Psalm Twenty-three to a man who, gazing intently and passionately upward, seems to be looking at something I can't see as he whispers the psalm's familiar words under his breath.

But what I see most of all when I look at this picture is a man who has nothing—yet not a word of complaint or pity leaves his mouth; I see a young girl who has everything and desires with all of her heart to give something to this man, but ends up receiving so much more than she could possibly have given away. I see the one object that has sustained this man over the years. It's that old, worn book on the chest. It is his Bible. That old book with its yellow, torn pages is his strength, encouragement, comfort, and his promise of an unimaginably perfect life in heaven with the One he loves and the One who loves him even more.

As I read Ellen's essay, I offered a silent prayer that whether young or old, we will always be sensitive to people's needs and will allow the love of Christ to flow through us to them.

Steps to Giving Yourself Away

1. Take time to count your blessings and give thanks to God.
2. Don't ever take for granted the gifts of life, health, security, family, friends, and faith.
3. Train yourself to stay sensitive to the needs of

others. Learn to see others' loneliness, fear, hopelessness, uncertainty, and pain. You won't be able to solve all their problems, but you can offer them the gifts of respect and understanding.

4. Begin to look for ways to give yourself away. Give a smile, a word of appreciation or encouragement, or an attitude of acceptance, as well as more tangible gifts such as money, food, or work.

5. Let the act of giving yourself away become your habit. As this happens, you will experience joy and agree with Jesus that "it is more blessed to give than to receive" (Acts 20:35).

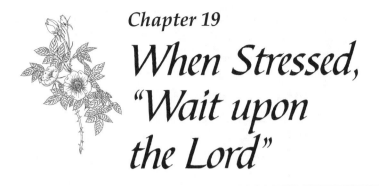

Chapter 19

When Stressed, "Wait upon the Lord"

They that wait upon the Lord shall renew their strength; they shall mount up with wings as eagles; they shall run, and not be weary; and they shall walk, and not faint.

—*Isaiah 40:31 (KJV)*

*T*ake two aspirin, drink a glass of warm milk, read the Twenty-third Psalm, and go to bed." This was a prescription reportedly given by a London doctor during World War II. It was a time when London was under almost constant bombing attack. People were frustrated, stressed, and frightened. Often they went days without sleep. Their nerves were on edge, and doctors' offices were jammed.

When I read about this, I recalled a 1987 report from the Mayo Clinic, which stated that fear, worry, hate, selfishness, and the inability to adjust to the world of reality were largely the causes of their patients' stomach illnesses, including ulcers.

I once heard an American doctor say on a TV newscast that as high as 70 percent of all patients who go to physicians could cure themselves if they could get rid of their fears and worries. This doesn't mean that psychosomatic illnesses are imaginary. Anyone who has suffered from migraine headaches or nervous indigestion knows that it's not just "in your mind." Yet there is a body of evidence indicating that persons suffering from the most serious illnesses can trace the onset of the illness to an emotional upset or trauma in which they felt powerless or hopeless.

Evidently, the Greek philosopher Plato, who lived twenty-three centuries ago, believed this, for he wrote, "The greatest mistake that physicians make is that they attempt to cure the body without attempting to cure the mind; yet the body and the mind are one and should not be treated separately." Perhaps this also is what Jesus meant when he said, "You shall love the Lord your God with all your heart [emotions], and with all your soul [spirit], and with all your mind [intellect]" (Matthew 22:37).

The management of stress in today's fast-paced, pressure-filled world may be one of our biggest needs if we are to live successfully and influentially. How do we do this? Let's take a second look at the British doctor's prescription. In essence, he was saying that we should use help from the medical community when we are ill. The aspirin is symbolic of that. Then we should use common sense and take care of our bodies. Drinking warm milk and going to bed represent that. Finally, we should allow the peace and power of faith to restore our souls. The Twenty-third Psalm is symbolic of that.

Another effective way to manage stress is to have a sense of humor. As the late Norman Cousins explained in his book *The Anatomy of an Illness*, a sense of humor clears your perspective, exercises your "insides," improves circulation, and makes you a much nicer person to know. In other words, humor alleviates stress. Having a humorous outlook on life actually can improve your health!

Similarly, having a positive attitude and thinking positive thoughts can help us to alleviate stress. We all know it to be true in our own lives: Our thoughts and attitudes really do affect our physical bodies. As the scripture tells us, "As [a man or woman] thinketh in his [or her] heart, so *is* he [or she]" (Proverbs 23:7 KJV). A long-held grudge doesn't really hurt the person against whom we carry the grudge, but it will give *us* headaches and stomachaches and will lower our resistance to disease. And if we allow our anger to go unchecked, it will grow. Often we say that a person is "blind with rage." This is an apt description of anger that is hardened into rage or hatred. It clouds our thinking, making it impossible to be objective, fair, or unprejudiced. We become obsessed with our rage, even paranoid in our actions. So, it is absolutely true that our thoughts and attitudes affect our physical health. They can bring about relaxation or stress.

Another way we can deal with stress is to stay focused on our goals. Giving in to the interruptions that are so prevalent in our everyday lives leaves us feeling fragmented, distracted, and overwhelmed. It was Peter Drucker, a well-known business consultant, who gave me a startlingly new idea about goals. At a seminar I attended, he said that before we set short- or long-term goals, we should determine our ultimate goals; that is, where we want to be when we "get there." After much soul-searching and adjusting, I came up with four succinct goals for my own life. I strongly recommend this exercise for you. It will put you in touch with the deep desires of your heart. I have learned that we can't focus on too many goals at once or we experience fragmentation and pressure. Our short-term and long-term goals should move us toward our ultimate goals.

Most important to managing stress is rooting and grounding our lives in eternal realities. For me, this means the Christian faith. It is not just a one-time commitment; it is a lifetime commitment to live in fellowship with the One who refreshes and empowers us. The prophet Isaiah said it beautifully many centuries ago: "They that wait upon the Lord shall renew their strength; they shall mount up with wings as eagles; they shall run, and not be weary; and they shall walk, and not faint" (Isaiah 40:31 KJV).

Steps to Handling Stress

1. Realize that just as there is good cholesterol and bad cholesterol, so also there is good stress (eustress) and bad stress (distress). All of us need a certain amount of stress to motivate us to reach our peak performance. Otherwise, we would be like soft, squishy marshmallows. Most of us do better with goals, plans, and even deadlines.
2. Practice these ways to help you avoid stress or handle it successfully:
• Stay physically fit.
• Plan "mini-vacations" or relaxing breaks during each day—and real vacations at least once a year.
• Don't play the blame game. Take responsibility for your life.
• Be positive.
• Don't overspend.
• Don't procrastinate.
• Learn to laugh easily.
• Learn new ways of thinking. In each stressful situation, ask yourself: What are my options here?
• Plan your week on Sunday afternoon or evening.
• Learn to say "no" without feeling guilty.

- Find someone with whom you can talk over your problems.
- Cultivate a "calm center" by having a quiet time daily to think; read inspirational materials, including the Bible; and pray.
- "Trust in the Lord with all your heart, and do not rely on your own insight. In all your ways acknowledge him, and he will make straight your paths" (Proverbs 3:5-6).

Chapter 20

Keep On Keeping On

Let us not grow weary in doing what is right, for we will reap at harvest time, if we do not give up.

—Galatians 6:9

I have been to hell and back," she answered in reply to my question and comment: "Where have you been? I have missed you." Though her eyes were smiling, it was obvious from the wheelchair in which she sat and the walker stationed nearby that "Amanda" had experienced a terrible trauma.

Immediately my mind went back several years ago to the day when I had seen a newspaper picture of her with the caption "Designer to the Queen." The article told about the beautiful gown she had designed and hand-sewn for that year's local beauty queen. The gown was on display and was exquisite in every detail—from the fine fabric to the unusual design and meticulous attention to details. It was then that I first had met Amanda and had learned that she was not only a designer but also a supervisor of difficult alterations for her customers.

It was in the latter position that her traumatic experience began. She was seated at her work station in the late afternoon when she had an excruciating pain comparable to a knife piercing her heart. She ran out into the store, saying, "I think I am having a heart attack. Will someone take me to the doctor?" Since neither the manager nor assistant manager were on the floor at that moment, one of the part-time workers volunteered to drive her.

Once inside the doctor's office, she was given medication to ease the pain; and after numerous tests, she was told that there was nothing wrong with her heart. It was the third doctor, an internist, who ordered the MRI after searching for trouble in her abdomen; and it was the MRI that led to the discovery of an aneurysm in the thoracic descending aorta. A surgeon was called. He said to Amanda: "This is extremely serious. If you are to live, we will have to operate immediately. If we operate, you will be paralyzed, but there is a 50 percent possibility that you will regain use of your lower body. The decision is yours."

"How long did it take you to ma+e the decision?" I asked. "About one minute," she replied. I couldn't begin to imagine what it meant to be totally paralyzed from the waist down. When she awakened after surgery, she couldn't turn herself, move her legs, or get out of bed. In fact, she said to her children, "The operation was a success, but the patient died." In her total helplessness, something seemed to have died within her.

For the first two weeks after her surgery, she didn't want to live. Yet, despite her despair, there was something in this remarkable woman's spirit that would not allow her to wallow long in self-pity. After self-pity came anger and a determination to "make myself walk again," she told me. Even these negative emotions allowed her to be more cooperative with the therapists. The real turning point in her recovery came when she asked some quadriplegics how they could be happy and laugh so much. They even worked out strenuously each day, though there was little likelihood they would ever regain full use of their limbs. A woman named Susan replied, "I pray a lot. Amanda, we are praying for you. Our prayer is that you can handle your pain without too much medication and that God will show you how to use all your strength and all your mind."

Amanda started to tell them that she didn't believe in God, that she felt the Bible was written about people and events of long ago and had nothing to do with today, and that people who believe in the Bible are only superstitious. Yet she could look at these people and know they had found resources far beyond their own—and beyond the medical help they had received. Alone that night, she again experienced excruciating pain, and in her terrible frustration she began to pray to "their God": "O God, if you are really there, and if it is your will, please let Susan's prayer for me be answered. Please let me help myself as much as possible." She told me that after saying that prayer, she began to feel herself growing calm inside, and that she even could tell that her blood pressure had dropped.

Some time later, she began to try to dress herself. "I would begin at 5:00 A.M. in order to be able to start the day at seven," she said. "It was when I could finally lift myself from the bed to the chair that I knew that I would walk again." Hope and faith began to rise in her spirit. "Their God" had become "her God."

Amanda has been faithful both in faith and persistence. Weekly she goes to a rehabilitation center for therapy. She has been able to return to work with the help of her wheelchair and a walker, and she is sure that some day she will walk with only the use of a cane. For this remarkable recovery, she gives credit to the medical community, to the rehabilitation centers, to her supportive family, to her own will to walk, and more than all of these, to her newfound faith in God.

Remember that you are never alone. God is closer than hands and feet. Our job is to have faith and to "keep on keeping on." As the apostle Paul reminds us in Romans 8:28, "All things [can] work together for good for those who love God, who are called according to his purpose."

Steps for How to Keep on Keeping On

1. Remember Forrest Gump's now famous quotation: "Life is like a box of chocolates. You never know what you're gonna get." As Christians, we believe that Forrest Gump's philosophy is both true and false. It is true in that life *is* full of surprises, both good and bad. But we do not believe that because something bad happens, our lives will be ruined. Instead, we believe with Paul: "We know that all things work together for good for those who love God, who are called according to his purpose" (Romans 8:28).

2. When something bad happens, let yourself feel the hurt in the situation. Don't deny the experience—whether it be an accident, the diagnosis of serious illness, the death of a loved one, the pain of divorce, the betrayal of a friend, the rebellion of a child, a natural loss, or some other difficult circumstance. *Experience* the grief.

3. Then look for options—God's options. Write them down—pros and cons. God expects us to use the minds he has given us.

4. Pray for guidance and expect to receive it.

5. Remember that you are never alone. God is closer than hands and feet; closer than breathing.

6. Remember that it is your job to "keep on keeping on." Or, as Dr. E. Stanley Jones once said, "When you get to the end of your rope, tie a knot and hang on."

7. Realize that only in retrospect will you see how God, the Master Weaver, was able to weave the ugly experiences into your life and make the tapestry beautiful. In the words of the song "Something Beautiful" by Bill and Gloria Gaither: "All I had to offer him was brokenness and strife, but he made something beautiful of my life."

Chapter 21

Take Hope with You into Every Day

Why are you cast down, O my soul, and why are you disquieted within me? Hope in God; for I shall again praise him, my help and my God.

—*Psalm 42:11*

*L*ife is full of dead-end streets. At least they seem to be dead-end streets. When we encounter these experiences—such as the loss of loved ones, the loss of a job, the end of a relationship, financial reverses, life-threatening illnesses—we feel trapped and hopeless. The temptation is to give up, quit, and lose hope. When we do this, we lower our resistance to disease, lose our creativity, and lose our will to win.

Several years ago in the science section of the *New York Times*, Daniel Goleman wrote an article entitled "Hope Emerges as Key to Success in Life." He said: "Psychologists are finding that hope plays a surprisingly important role in giving people a measurable advantage in realms as diverse as academic achievement, bearing up in difficult jobs, and coping with serious illness."

That statement certainly was proven true in my own life. It was early March 1991. The tests were completed; the surgery was scheduled; now I was waiting in my hospital room for the doctor to come by with final instructions. There was apprehension in my heart as I waited. The tests had indicated that the ovarian tumor was large, and that it was pushing against other organs in my body and must be removed. What we didn't know was whether or not there was a malignancy.

When the doctor walked into my hospital room, some of my anxieties subsided. His very presence brought assurance. Even his voice seemed to say that whatever happened, everything was going to be all right. I relaxed as he told me what to expect the following day—from the kind of anesthesia to be used to the options he would have when he saw the tumor. If the tumor seemed to be self-contained and the immediate pathology report looked good, then I would be in surgery less than two hours and would return to my hospital room. If the tumor proved to be malignant and the cancer had spread to other organs, then the surgery would take longer and I would be taken to the Intensive Care Unit afterward.

The following day when I began to awaken from the anesthesia, it was obvious that I was not in my hospital room. Nurses were hovering, and I could hear the sound of life-sustaining machines. In addition, I seemed to have tubes coming out of every organ of my body. My heart sank. Hope vanished. Yet momentarily, when my vision cleared, I could see my husband and son standing on one side of my bed and my doctor on the other side— and they were smiling.

In a strong, confident voice, my doctor said: "There was a malignancy, but I think we were able to get it all. As a precaution, however, you will take nine or ten months of chemotherapy, and then we will have second-look surgery. I am sure you are going to be fine." My heart began to soar.

Webster defines hope as "a feeling of desire accompanied by anticipation and expectation." The desire to be well had been there all along, but it became hope when the doctor gave me reason to anticipate it. Hope was a light, buoyant feeling that enabled me to sing despite pain and tubes and the prospect of chemotherapy.

Obviously, hope is much deeper than just a feeling. The apostle Paul suggests in the thirteenth chapter of 1 Corinthians that we have three things to equip us for daily living: "And now faith, hope, and love abide" (v. 13). And theologian Emil Brunner once wrote, "What oxygen is to the lungs, hope is to the meaning of life."

My husband and I had the privilege of visiting and writing about some of the fastest-growing churches throughout the United States. One of those was Metropolitan United Methodist Church on Woodward Avenue in Detroit, Michigan. On the lawn in front of the church is the statue of a nameless man about forty years of age. The story is told that during the depression, Dr. Merton Rice preached an unforgettable sermon on hope. In the congregation of discouraged people that day was a notable artist. He was so impressed with the sensible message of undefeated faith and hope that he hurried to his studio and molded the statue that stands on the church lawn. It depicts a man struggling in adversity—his muscles straining in exertion to overcome. On the base of the statue is inscribed the scripture upon which Dr. Rice's sermon was based: "Why art thou cast down, O my soul? and why art thou disquieted within me? hope thou in God: for I shall yet praise him, who is the health of my countenance, and my God" (Psalm 42:11 KJV).

Take hope with you into every day of your life!

Steps to Taking Hope with You

1. Remember that losing hope lowers your resistance to disease, sidetracks your creativity, and deprives you of motivation.

2. Remember, on the other hand, that having hope gives you a measurable advantage in achieving academic goals, holding steady in difficult situations, and coping with serious illnesses.

3. Think of a time when the power of hope sustained you in a difficult circumstance. Relive the experience in your mind. Then, give thanks that God is giving you hope as part of your spiritual equipment.

4. Repeat biblical affirmations and use them throughout the day as needed. Some appropriate ones include the following:

• "Hope is the anchor of the soul" (Hebrews 6:19, author's paraphrase).

• "The God of love and peace will be with you" (2 Corinthians 13:11).

• "Hope in God; for I shall again praise him, my help and my God" (Psalm 42:11).

Chapter 22

Believe in Angels

An angel of the Lord appeared to him in a dream and said, "Joseph, son of David, do not be afraid to take Mary as your wife, for the child conceived in her is from the Holy Spirit."

—Matthew 1:20

One year during the week before Christmas, Kathy Stone was distraught about a court case in which she was involved. One day as she left her attorney's office in the Republic Centre, she dissolved in tears. Though she was wearing sunglasses when she entered the elevator, tears were streaming down her cheeks.

"There was an angel on that elevator," Kathy told me during a telephone conversation. She continued to describe the angel:

> Joanna was a beautiful, African American young woman in her early twenties who was on her way down from the Walden Club. A student at the University of Tennessee at Chattanooga, she had the most dazzling smile that enveloped me in its warmth.
>
> Sensing my need, she talked quietly and encouragingly to me, saying things like, "Don't be discouraged. God will take care of you." By the time she had walked me to my car, my entire perspective had changed. I had moved from despair to hope; from confusion to clarity in my thinking. As I drove home, I said to myself: "Kathy, I think you have just had a visit from a Christmas angel."

As I reflected on our conversation, I thought about the continuing interest in angels these days. For many years, there was little written on the subject, but now bookstores are filled with "angel books" and all kinds of angel merchandise, such as angel pins, angel cards, and angel calendars. Even television has capitalized on the interest. Like many others, I have enjoyed the delightful television series *Touched by an Angel*, starring Roma Downey as Angel Monica and Della Reese as Tess, the head angel. They are sent to protect, guide, encourage, and comfort human beings who are struggling with real-life situations. It is a program that emphasizes strong moral values and religious faith.

What is an angel? Webster defines an angel as "a messenger from God; a supernatural being characterized by more than human power of influence; a guiding spirit or influence." The Bible teaches us that God's Holy Spirit has been given to guide and empower us. In addition, the Bible indicates—in nearly three hundred different places—that God has countless angels at his command. Although the Bible doesn't give us much *specific* information about angels, it does say that they will be a source of comfort and strength in every kind of circumstance.

In his book *Angels*, Dr. Billy Graham describes angels as "created spirit beings who can become visible when necessary." As I look back on my own life, I realize that the many angels—messengers of God—who have blessed my life have all been visible and known to me. I seldom have dreamed of loved ones who have died, but once when I needed to make an important decision and my usual methods had not worked, my mother, who had died years earlier, appeared in my dream and said two sentences that enabled me to see things in clear perspective. At other times in my life when I have needed a word of encouragement or hope, or when I have needed help with a difficult situation, these messengers of God have appeared in the form of friends or family members. When it happens, I always remember these lines:

When God comes to me on quiet, cat-like feet,
Why am I surprised that it is my neighbor down the street?

I have read many documented angel stories, including the story about the British express train that was carrying Queen Victoria and was stopped short of a washed-out bridge by a "winged figure"; and the one about Eddie Rickenbacker, who believed an angel provided food for him and his B-17 crew, enabling them to survive for weeks on a life raft in the Pacific. But none is more compelling than a story carried in the *Reader's Digest* in the mid-1970s.

According to the story, a celebrated Philadelphia neurologist had gone to bed after a very tiring day. Suddenly, he was awakened by someone knocking on his door. Upon opening it, he found a little girl, poorly dressed and very upset. She told him her mother was ill and asked if he would please come with her. It was a bitterly cold, snowy night; and though he was exceptionally tired, the doctor dressed and followed the girl. He found the mother desperately ill with pneumonia. After providing for medical care, he complimented the sick woman on the intelligence and persistence of her little daughter. The woman looked at him strangely and said, "My daughter died a month ago." She added, "Her shoes and coat are in the clothes closet there." Amazed and perplexed, the doctor went to the closet and opened the door. There hung the very coat worn by the little girl who had brought him to attend to her mother. It was warm and dry and could not possibly have been worn on that wintry night. The story went on to say that in the intervening years, the doctor had wondered if he had been called in the hour of desperate need by an angel who appeared as the woman's young daughter.

Whenever we are reminded of angels—through a story, a song, a book, a television show, or something else—let us remember that we are not alone on planet Earth. The good news of the Christian faith is that God, through Christ, is with us. His messengers, in varying forms, will be dispatched to guide, protect, and comfort us. "Glory to God in the highest" (Luke 2:14)!

Steps to Enable You to Believe in Angels

1. See for yourself what the Bible has to say about angels. There are nearly three hundred passages referring to angels, such as this one from the book of Luke: "For it is written, 'He will command his angels concerning you, to protect you'" (4:10). Consult a Bible concordance to locate other verses, or read one of the many excellent resource books on the subject.

2. If you agree that angels are "messengers from God," then give thanks every day for people who help, encourage, comfort, and support you. They are your "angels unaware" (see Hebrews 13:2).

3. Realize that you can be "God's messenger" for others. Look for opportunities to serve and help others in the name of Christ.

4. Don't let the logic of your mind rule out the possibility of angels. I like Dr. Billy Graham's descrip-

tion of angels as "created spirit beings who can become visible when necessary."

5. Don't become obsessed with looking for evidence of angels or "spirit beings." Remember that the good news is that God loves us, has redeemed us through Christ, and empowers us through the ultimate angel: the Holy Spirit, who guides and directs our lives if we allow it.

Chapter 23

Become a Geriatric Gypsy

The LORD said to Abram, "Go from your country and your kindred and your father's house to the land that I will show you. I will make of you a great nation."

—Genesis 12:1-2a

While on a trip out West, my husband and I were having dinner with a group of senior adults, all of whom enjoy traveling. In fact, at that meal, each person was describing his or her favorite trip. Suddenly, a vivacious woman with soft, neatly coifed gray hair said, "We are just a bunch of geriatric gypsies."

Webster defines *gypsy* as someone who looks like, lives like, or wanders like the Indo-European people known throughout the world as gypsies. It was our obvious delight in wandering the earth to which our friend referred. Since that day I have considered the many benefits of being a "geriatric gypsy." Let me pause here to say that even if you are young, the habits you are forming now will determine whether you end your life as a rigid, negative, unhappy person or as a "geriatric gypsy."

The first benefit that comes to mind is that travel—whether we are going to a town ten miles from us or to another section of the country or world—keeps us from being too set in our ways. My observation is that as we get older, it is easy for us to become rigid, inflexible, and unwilling to change. Some people don't even like to sleep in a different bed or eat unfamiliar foods. If we aren't careful, our world can become smaller, our conversation shallow, and our focus self-centered.

Even if travel is not possible for us at this time, we can become "geriatric gypsies" in our spirits. We can learn new things, remain concerned about community and world events, and stay involved with friends, hobbies, and church. Whatever happens, we need to avoid ruts and "shake up" our thinking. When we learn to laugh at ourselves and do something to serve others, our lives are far more exciting.

I have an older friend—the politically correct term these days is not "older" but "chronologically gifted"—who is one of the most alive persons I know. When Melissa's husband, John, died several years ago, her friends were afraid that she would retreat into a shell. Melissa and John had been extremely close, but he had been the dynamic, "take charge" one of the duo. Somehow we had perceived her as sweet and likable yet rather dependent. After John's death, Melissa had a few bad months in which there were many adjustments, followed by the usual longer period of grief. After that, however, she surprised us all. In addition to accepting responsibility for planning trips for the seniors at her church, she began to deliver meals-on-wheels and to work with hospice. "I did this," she said, "because I remembered two things. In his book *In One Ear and Out the Other*, Sam Levenson wrote: 'We are given two hands—one to help ourselves and one to help others.' Also, I remembered Jesus' words: 'Inasmuch as ye have done it unto one of the least of these my brethren, ye have done it unto me'" (Matthew 25:40 KJV).

More than anything else, Melissa stunned us by learning a new hobby: whitewater rafting. When asked about this, she said, "I am tired of being a settler; I want to be a pioneer. Besides, I don't have too many more years on this earth. As Justice Oliver Wendell Holmes said when asked about his learning Greek when he was ninety: 'It's now or never.'" There's no doubt about it: Melissa has bounce-back ability!

There is another thing I like about being a "geriatric gypsy." We seem to celebrate wherever we are. In every picture I have seen of gypsies, they too are celebrating by dancing or singing. Because the golden years bring some restrictions and more aches and pains, there is a temptation to complain and to look on the gloomy side. We have to make a conscious effort to be positive, to see humor in everyday experiences, and to enjoy life wherever we are. I believe this comes from counting our blessings rather than focusing on our problems; from remembering what we have left and not what we have lost. A wonderful daily affirmation comes from the twenty-fourth verse of Psalm 118: "This is the day which the LORD hath made; let us rejoice and be glad in it." Indeed, whatever age we may be, *let us rejoice!*

Steps to Becoming a Geriatric Gypsy

1. Even if you are young, realize that the habits you are forming now will determine whether you end your life as a rigid, negative, unhappy person or a geriatric gypsy.
2. Stay flexible: Try new foods; make friends in different age groups; drive a different way to work or church every now and then.

3. If you are unhappy about a situation, do what you can to change it or change your attitude. Don't get in the habit of complaining! Even your voice will become whiny. It is a sure way to lose friends.

4. Travel as often as you can. Learn to appreciate different cultures. You don't have to agree with a philosophy of a culture to appreciate and respect the people who live in that place.

5. Try to learn something new every day. Television, newspapers, books (especially inspirational books), travelogues—your resources are unlimited.

6. Learn to laugh more easily, especially at yourself.

7. Stay involved with friends, hobbies, church, and community activities.

8. Always stay interested in people. Even if you can't get out often, you can telephone people to congratulate them or to share sympathy with them.

9. Pray for others daily.

10. Don't become self-centered.

Chapter 24

Turn Tragedy into Triumph

We know that all things work together for good for those who love God, who are called according to his purpose.

—Romans 8:28

*F*inal exams were just completed for the fall quarter of 1983, and students of the University of Alabama would be going home for Christmas the following day. Lundy Mills and a few of her friends in her apartment complex got together to share hors d'oeuvres and to exchange Christmas gifts.

"I'm still hungry," one of the guys declared. "Lundy, let me borrow your car so I can get a hamburger." As was her custom when someone asked to borrow her car, she replied jauntily, "You can drive the car, but I'll go with you." Her friend had eaten his hamburger and they were almost back to the campus when the accident occurred. Suddenly a car, occupied by two freshmen who had had their celebration at a bar, hit Lundy's car broadside, causing them to make a 360-degree turn. Lundy, who was sitting on the passenger side, was thrown through the window into a telephone pole; her leg, still inside the car, was crushed when the impact pushed the engine like a crumpled toy into the passenger space.

"My miracles began immediately," Lundy later told me as we ate lunch together at a restaurant. From our table we could see the Tennessee River flowing lazily and peacefully only a few yards from us. The scene was a sharp contrast to the tumultuous emotions racing through me as I heard the story of a tragic accident and the beauty of God's grace and watchful care.

The collision of the two cars was so great that one hit an electrical transformer and lights were knocked out throughout the area. Upon hearing the crash, a man who lived nearby and worked at a local hospital was the first one on the scene. Fortunately, he knew to hold Lundy up to keep her from drowning in her own blood until she could be extricated from the wreckage.

The paramedics lifted her out of the car with their "jaws of life" equipment and placed her in mast trousers to elevate her blood pressure and get her circulation going. Even so, when she arrived at the emergency room of the hospital, she was brain-dead. Though medical personnel attended her wounds, no method of life support was used until her father signed a release when he arrived from Chattanooga at 3:30 A.M. Lundy told me that at one point doctors had put her on a gurney to be rolled to the morgue.

The accident occurred on Saturday night, and on Sunday morning her pastor, Dr. Ben Haden, had the entire congregation at the First Presbyterian Church praying for her. On Monday morning, brain waves were beginning to be registered, and in three days she came out of the coma. It was six weeks later before she was fully aware of what had happened. Her right side was paralyzed, her teeth were wired together, the right side of her face was crushed, her legs had multiple fractures, and her right eye was closed.

The concussion, caused by the terrific blow to Lundy's

head, resulted in damage to the frontal lobe of her brain. Short-term memory and emotions were affected. She could remember things that happened when she was a child, but the memory of things that had happened that day or that week seemed to fade into thin air. In addition, she had little control over her emotions, sometimes laughing or crying hysterically.

Lundy told me there were three things that got her through those trying days. First was the deep belief that she, eventually, would be well. Second was the certain knowledge that God would be with her every step of the way. She knew that God would give her courage to face the future if she had enough faith to take the necessary next steps. Third, members of her family and friends were the support group she needed, encouraging her and giving her hope. She said that her mother was a wonderful blessing to her, and that a close friend constantly pointed the way for her.

Lundy's courage was obvious from the first time she was able to be up all day. She soon began going out in public, especially to church. She did this despite the fact that her jaws were held together by wires (this facial surgery collapsed, necessitating a second facial reconstruction).

It was courage and determination that led Lundy back to the University of Alabama in August of 1984. Her doctors and members of her family were afraid that it was too soon, but Lundy wanted desperately to complete her education. It was not easy! Having been an honor student, she was stunned when she received a grade of 30 on her first test. Little by little, her cognitive and writing skills returned, and she graduated in May 1985.

"Did you ever ask 'why' or lose hope?" I asked the poised young woman who sat across from me.

She replied thoughtfully, "I never blamed God, and only once did I get discouraged enough to ask 'why.' There is no doubt that God gave me the patience and strength that I needed." Then she added, "Throughout this entire experience, I have seen many miracles—from a hospital attendant finding us and knowing what to do; to the paramedics who knew to put me in mast trousers to elevate blood pressure; to our being led in unusual ways to find the right doctors, especially for the six surgeries; to my college graduation."

As I looked at this courageous young woman who now works in a family business and is active in church, Junior League, and civic affairs, I concluded: "Lundy, the greatest miracle is that you are alive and whole and able, through God's help, to turn your tragedy into triumph."

Steps to Turning Your Tragedy into Triumph

1. Remember that we live in an imperfect world. We are no longer in the Garden of Eden. All of us live, as John Steinbeck says in his novel of a similar name, "East of Eden." Jesus told us that "in this world you will have trouble" (John 16:33 NIV). We will cause some of our problems and tragedies, but some will be caused by others' actions or by circumstances beyond our control.
2. Knowing this, you never need to ask "Why?" or "Why *me*?" A more appropriate question might be "Why *not* me?" After all, we all have received incredible blessings, and I doubt that we stop and ask "Why me?" when these good things happen.

3. If you are committed to Christ and seek to live in God's purposes, you can be sure of several things:

• God can use what he did not choose! In Romans 8:28, Paul expresses this thought with these words: "And we know that all things work together for good for those who love God, who are called according to his purpose."

• God will never leave you or forsake you. In Matthew 28:20, Jesus tells us, "And remember, I am with you always, to the end of the age."

• No matter how hopeless the situation seems or how severe the pain, you are not alone. Through God's power and presence, you can overcome any difficulty.

4. Walk *through* the difficulty, using all the resources at your disposal, do your best, and then trust God for the rest.

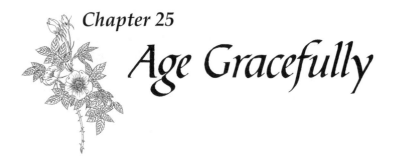

Chapter 25

Age Gracefully

She is clothed with strength and dignity; she can laugh at the days to come.

—*Proverbs 31:25 (NIV)*

Margaret Skeete of Radford, Virginia, lived to be 113 years old and was included in the *Guinness Book of World Records*. I first met her in 1982, when I spoke at a women's meeting in her town. In the business session preceding my speech, Lil Bondurant asked for a matter of special privilege. She wanted to honor one of the two hundred women present.

When the honoree stood, I thought, "What a lovely looking elderly woman." She was petite and immaculately groomed. Her coral-colored suit softened and enlivened her face. Her gray hair was beautifully coifed.

In the presentation, Lil Bondurant expressed gratitude for Margaret Skeete's active participation in church and community groups; for her happy, optimistic attitude; for her caring concern for others; and for her delightful sense of humor. Then came the shocker: Margaret Skeete was 104 years old at the time!

I couldn't believe what I was hearing. This was no "little old lady in tennis shoes." I learned later that she always wears high heels and dresses or skirts, still makes her own clothes (all in bright colors—she doesn't like dark colors), puts on make-up every morning, and is always well groomed. I also learned that she had grown up in Texas and had been a dressmaker in Houston. Her first husband had died after two years of marriage. A number of years later, she had married a rancher, Reen T. Skeete, and they had moved to San Angelo, Texas. They had had two children, a son and a daughter. Following the death of her second husband, Margaret had moved to Radford to live with her daughter.

As I think of this remarkable woman and others who have lived beyond the biblical "three score and ten years," I wonder what is the secret of their longevity. More important, what is the secret of aging *gracefully*? Nobody wants to be a cantankerous, complaining old person. Such persons create unhappiness for themselves and torment for close relatives and friends.

Through my observation of Margaret Skeete and others who have aged gracefully, I have concluded that they have several things in common. First, they take good care of themselves. They eat nutritionally, exercise, and take a vitamin supplement especially formulated for older adults. In short, they stay active and keep those muscles moving.

Second, they think "right." There is no "hardening of attitudes" for these people. They are interested in what is going on now in the world. They are not obsessed with the past or unduly concerned about the future. They are in touch with today.

Third, they are disciplined. Like Margaret Skeete, they provide structure for their lives; they get out of bed each day, get dressed, and begin to execute a plan. A friend of mine told me that her mother taught piano when she was in her eighties. One day her mother said, "If I give in to my feelings, I'll stay in bed today; but I won't." That's discipline!

Fourth, they have chosen to be happy and to live with hope. By the time you have lived to be eighty or ninety or one hundred, you have had some hard experiences in life. We, too, have our own share of difficulties, but we can choose to be happy "in spite of" these experiences. This kind of choice makes for personal serenity and pleasant interpersonal relationships.

Finally, those who age gracefully have learned to live according to the wisdom of this proverb: "Trust in the Lord with all your heart, and do not rely on your own insight" (Proverbs 3:5). As the average life expectancy continues to increase, perhaps our prayer should not be for more years, but for more life in the years we have!

Steps to Aging Gracefully

1. Anticipate and look forward to your senior years.

2. Decide that you are not going to be a whining, complaining old person. So much of this is a choice—a daily choice.

3. Resolve not to talk about your physical problems, and begin the habit now. Other people aren't interested in hearing about them, and it only makes you feel worse to talk about them. A beautiful older woman once told me: "As my aches and pains become more numerous, I have a strong temptation to give an 'organ recital' to my friends. I resist the temptation because I do want a few friends left at the end of my life."

4. Don't allow "hardening of the attitudes," at

least of bad attitudes, because they become habitual. Cultivate positive attitudes, such as gratitude, magnanimity, and compassion.

5. Stay engaged with life. Talk to friends regularly; keep up with what's happening in your community and in the world. As long as you are physically able, participate in social events and family, church, and community activities.

6. Live in the present, not the past, and look forward to the future.

7. Let Proverbs 3:5-6 be your motto: "Trust in the Lord with all your heart, and do not rely on your own insight. In all your ways acknowledge him, and he will make straight your paths."

8. Believe in these lines from Robert Browning's poem "Rabbi Ben Ezra": "[Come,] grow old along with me! The best is yet to be . . . ."

Chapter 26

Remember That You Are Chosen

"Ye have not chosen me, but I have chosen you, and ordained you, that ye should go and bring forth fruit."
—*John 15:16 (KJV)*

---

*L*ook at the snow on the mountains," I said as my husband and I awakened and looked out over nature's "down comforter" that June day in Oberammergau. It was our first trip to the small German village where for four hundred years the villagers have put on the Passion Play, depicting the life, passion, death, and resurrection of Jesus Christ. Actually, the play is presented every ten years because of a pledge the villagers made to God in gratitude for being spared during the terrible plague that killed millions of Europeans in 1618.

Four years before each presentation, the actors and actresses are elected by adult members of the village. This gives them sufficient time to grow long hair or beards and prepare mentally and spiritually for the biblical characters they will portray. Because there are not enough hotel rooms to accommodate the thousands of visitors who come six nights each week during the months of May through September, one half of the homes in the village become "bed and breakfast" inns for the tourists.

We chose to stay in a bed and breakfast, and we were fortunate enough to be in the home of the woman who played Mary Magdalene in the drama. She prepared our breakfast before she bicycled down to the auditorium where the longest (once eight hours and now six hours in duration, with a luncheon break) live drama in the world was presented. She also provided blankets to keep us warm, since the stage area is open and cold mountain air moves quickly through the unheated auditorium.

It was thrilling that morning to walk with the crowds toward the large auditorium located in the center of the Alpine village. Visitors from many countries were talking excitedly about the drama they had heard or read so much about. Then, promptly at 8:30 A.M., the chorus that preceded each act marched onto the spacious stage, and a quiet fell over the audience. Though the play is in German, we knew the story so well that we never had to refer to the English translation given to us.

At about 3:00 in the afternoon, when the cross was being raised in the crucifixion scene, a sudden thunderstorm occurred. There was thunder and lightning, and then darkness covered the landscape. It was so eerie and realistic that when Jesus spoke from the cross, I felt he was speaking directly to me. I had read about the crucifixion all of my life, but that day I experienced it. I understood the price Christ had paid for my redemption. It must have had a similar effect upon others, because five thousand people walked out of the auditorium without uttering a sound.

As a follower of Christ, I had never felt so unworthy. In retrospect, I realized that I had served Christ almost arrogantly, as if he were fortunate to have me as a disciple. I found myself weeping silently often during the next two days of our travel to Vienna. Once in our hotel there, my husband, Ralph, suggested that we go to

St. Stephen's Cathedral, located only a block from our hotel, to pray. I was more than ready! While I was praying silently in the cathedral, it happened. As clearly as I can hear others speak, I heard these words: "You have not chosen me, but I have chosen you and ordained you that you might bear much fruit." I knew that the words were scripture, but at that time I wasn't a good enough Bible student to know where to find them without looking them up in a concordance. After finding them in John 15:16 later that day, I wrote in the margin of my Bible: "My ordination in Vienna on June 25, 1970."

In the intervening years, when I have felt unworthy or inadequate for Christian service, I remember I am chosen by Christ and will be empowered to serve. These were his words not only to his disciples in Galilee, but also to contemporary believers such as you and me—who are called to share the message of Christ's love, forgiveness, hope, and joy in the twenty-first century. I challenge you to memorize John 15:16; to remember that you are chosen; and to receive your ordination as a servant of Christ in the new century.

Steps for Receiving Your Ordination as a Servant of Christ

1. Recognize that the world has a way of "whittling us down to size," and our own mental voices of doubt and perfectionism often make us feel inadequate. We need to remember God's unconditional love for us. Look up the word *love* in a Bible concordance, and see how often the Bible tells of God's love for us. Begin to internalize and truly accept the message.

2. When you feel unworthy or especially inadequate, remember that you *are* worthy, not because of what you have done, but because of what God has done for you through Christ (John 3:16).

3. Understand that God's love and blessings are given not only so that you may experience personal joy but also so that you may serve others in his name.

4. Receive your ordination and empowerment to serve by reading and claiming John 15:16.

5. Stay close to Christ and remain sensitive to the needs of others.